I0724860

# *The* Cinderella Monologues

**2nd edition**

*Inspiring Stories
of Women Finding
Courage & Success*

Collected by Mila Johansen

**Featuring 14 Amazing Women Authors**

Published by: Mila Johansen, Emerald Horse Publishing
Design & layout:  Mariah Miller Creative Services

Second edition: 2023
Paperback ISBN: 978-1-952508-12-7
Hardcover ISBN: 978-1-952508-13-4

*This book is dedicated to all women in the world
who have struggled and strived to create better lives
for themselves, their children and their families.*

*And to all the women who have dedicated their lives
to helping others on our small planet through encouragement,
teaching, volunteerism and counseling, giving tirelessly
of themselves to any cause that furthers the optimism
and hope of humankind.*

*We are all part of one planet and need to work together to
create harmony, acceptance, understanding and encouragement
for everyone of all faiths, cultures and hemispheres.*

# Table of Contents

**Mila Johansen** is a public speaker, writing and publishing coach, teacher and writer. She is the best-selling author of nine books, including *From Cowgirl to Congress: Journey of a Suffragist on the Front Lines*, a first-person account from Jessie Haver Butler, Mila's grandmother. Her first job was to help put together the Pulitzer School of Journalism. She was the first woman lobbyist in D.C. and taught public speaking to thousands of women including Eleanor Roosevelt. In her early 90s, Jessie shared the podium several times with Gloria Steinem and Marlo Thomas and took Mila along.

Mila also has several more books in progress and loves to write and produce short screenplays. She has developed "The Short Book" concept, giving people all over the world permission to write and publish their "short book" first.

Now she is helping many people write and publish their books, making the process easy and accessible. She loves to work in any genre, including fiction, memoirs, anthologies and cookbooks, making people's dreams of becoming published authors come true.

Email: johansenmila@gmail.com
Website: milajohansen.com

# Introduction
## by Mila Johansen

*"Faith consists in believing when it is beyond
the power of reason to believe."*
-Voltaire

I often speak on podcasts and summits, around the world, about my journey from poverty to abundance as a real-life Cinderella. I am tied to Cinderella through my maiden name—Grimm. There are all sorts of "real" Cinderella stories out there. Almost every woman has one to tell, whether it comes from overcoming being bullied in school or at work, abusive family members or partners, life-threatening illnesses, or other adverse situations.

In all my Cinderella travels, I discovered what is thought to be one of the first "real" Cinderella stories in history. Rhodopis was a Greek slave girl who married the Pharaoh of Egypt. In the Egyptian version, the magical animal is an eagle who helps the Pharoah find Rhodopis by dropping her sandal into his lap. Instead of a cruel step-family, Rhodopis is enslaved and owned by cruel masters. The third pyramid at Giza is attributed to her.

There are life circumstances beyond our control, and beyond our imaginings, which create hardships that seem insurmountable. Abuses, illnesses, deaths of parents, loved ones, children, and other life challenges that seem extreme, and yet can make us stronger.

I speak about my experiences to inspire other women that no matter where they came from, or what has happened to them, they can do and be anything! When the idea came to me to invite other women to tell their stories, I had already been working on my memoir for the previous eight years with a working title of *The Cinderella Monologues*.

I also wrote a musical entitled *Ella, Cinderella* and produced it on the main stage in our community. In transforming my favorite story into a musical, I wanted it to have some of the depth of the movie *Ever After*, and yet show a lot of humor, to make it entertaining for stage. I worked hard to achieve that and accomplished the humorous parts with two comical fairies who serve the Fairy Godmother.

A woman who attended the production wrote me a touching letter that reached down into my core. It convinced me that *The Cinderella Monologues* needed to be an anthology of several womens' stories, not just my personal memoir. My own memoir is now entitled, *Cinderella Interrupted*.

The woman wrote me that she had been a "real" Cinderella and that my musical touched her deeply; she thanked me profusely. She told me her story, which made my Cinderella story look like a family sitcom from the 60s. She and her father were close, but he remarried the "Wicked Stepmother" who brought two daughters with her. The new mother made her do all the housework and even serve her and her daughters. Then her father died and the woman remarried a man who was even more abusive, in every way.

I cried as I read her story and knew immediately that I needed to help facilitate other women to tell their stories. I have taught writing and publishing for the past few decades and put together and published several anthologies during that time. So, I got excited and started inviting women to participate in this endeavor.

I have always been touched deeply by any Cinderella story no matter how trivial or well done. I always tear up—because of my own experience growing up as a "real" Cinderella. My favorite rendition is the movie, *Ever After*, I find myself watching it several times a year and call it "Cinderella with a bite!"

I now realize everything that happened to me built my character. Many of the events that took place in my life as a child, became the cornerstones of who I have become today. I was the Cinderella in our household. From the age of 10, I did all of the housework and much of the cooking for our family, spending about four hours a day.

I grew up in a very meager, poor home with a single mother. I often went to school without lunch and watched as all the kids who sat in front of me feasted on sack lunches. But I don't want anyone to feel sorry for me, because I later married a farmer and now have all the food I need. We donate 10,000 pounds, or more, per year of our organic citrus to local food banks. Through this story, I want to inspire people to go out and help children they know and see who may not have lunch, or a decent dinner.

Later, I found out that many of my friends had been abused. Back in those days, we didn't have talk shows to expose those kinds of travesties, so many women believed they were the only one, or that it was somehow their fault. As I grew older and heard these stories from women, I found out that 50% of my friends had been molested or raped.

When the "Me Too" movement came out, many more women I know told me they, too had fallen prey to abuse and the number rose to 75%. Shocking! Living with a single mom turned out to be very fortunate, because there were no men around to abuse me by proxy. I call that an abundance. I count my life in abundances.

As a feminist, I encourage women to speak out and report what happened to them, even if it happened long ago, even if it will ruin a family's life. One of the main reasons I tell women to speak out is so the perpetrator won't be able to abuse someone else.

My mother was a third-grade teacher, which is part of the reason I'm a teacher. She would leave at six in the morning and drive forty minutes to set up her classroom. Due to her long hours away from home, she didn't realize she had moved us into an unsavory and dangerous neighborhood. So, at a very young age, I had to get my brother up, make sure he got breakfast, and get us both out the door to walk a mile to school.

Bobby was two and a half years younger and his only chores were to take out the trash and mow the lawn of our tract home. In some ways, I think the lack of responsibility ruined him. He didn't make it out of our gangland upbringing. When we were very young, I remember we would often go to bed without dinner. Now I appreciate every single thing that is given to me.

Okay, I'm not ashamed to admit it—I am also a real-life "Pollyanna." I think the very first movie I saw in a theatre, at the age of seven, was *Pollyanna.* That one movie affected and is still affecting me, in so many ways. For one thing, I came home wishing there was a big screen on my bedroom wall so that I could watch *Pollyanna* any time I wanted. We didn't have a television in our home yet. I hadn't seen any other movie, except every Sunday night, we went across the street to my grandmother's house to watch Disney's *Sunday Night Movies*. Now, I think it's amazing that any of us can watch whatever we want at any time. I often still marvel about that.

So my life has been a lot like the "Pollyanna" attitude in the movie—"The Glad Game." At one point, she tells the story of a time with her father. Pollyanna wanted a doll, so her father said, "Let's go look in the church donation barrel." The only item they found that day was a pair of crutches. So he said, "Let's play the glad game. Let's think on something to be glad for about finding the crutches." Pollyanna thought for a minute and then said, "Well, I guess I can be glad I don't need the crutches."

That has been my attitude in life at so many times. For some reason, I've always thought I could have everything. I just had a feeling that my life was great and nothing seemed to get me down. Maybe I often went hungry, but I always remained positive. I must have been a "glass half-full" kind of girl, even back then. Now I give back in as many ways and in as many places I can. It's almost like a puzzle and is a lot of fun to do.

My famous suffragette grandmother Jessie Haver Butler became my "fairy godmother," providing me with lifelong tools and strategies I still use today. She took me under her fairy wings and encouraged me to find inspiration and fulfillment through my working endeavors. She taught me public speaking, how to write books, and to work hard for my dreams and make them a reality.

Jessie is the inspiration for this book, as a real-life Cinderella. She grew up on a Colorado cattle ranch where she suffered horrific tragedies and abuses, including incest and murder. First, her baby sister Francis died, followed by her mother three days later, leaving her with an impossible workload for a ten-year-old girl. Later, her stepmother and younger brother also perished. A teacher discovered how bright Jessie was and helped her get into Smith College. Against her father's will, she escaped her tragic home life and was soon thrust into the center of several worldwide events. She never looked back. She worked on the front lines in 1920 when women won the right to vote, as the first woman lobbyist at the Capitol in Washington D.C. Her story is your story of winning the right to vote.

I include part of her story, in her own words, at the end of this book, since she was the original inspiration. I published her memoir, *From Cowgirl to Congress*, in 2020 for the 100th anniversary of women in the U.S. winning the right to vote on August 18, 1920. In her late 90s, she often shared the podium with Gloria Steinem and Marlo Thomas and took me along.

Each story from this book's amazing authors represents what women have had to go through in centuries past, and what they are still going through now. Most people do not realize that women have been the most marginalized population all through history. What I find inspiring is the resilience, fortitude and creativity of each one of the women in this book, and how they overcame often unthinkable obstacles to become the amazing people they are today.

*~ Mila Johansen*

*"We have to reinvent ourselves
until the end."*

~ Oprah Winfrey

**Billy's Auntie** spent her early childhood years constantly nagging her parents to take her to see the bison herd owned by the city of Denver. In later years, trips to Yellowstone became a ritual.

After graduating from Arizona State University, she became a realtor, later forming real estate syndications. She advanced to become a developer, designing and building homes, as well as office warehouse and mini-storage facilities.

Upon moving to the San Francisco Bay area, The Auntie started the widely published interior design firm, Kathy Monteiro Designer and Associates, in which she is still involved today, doing work there and in Grass Valley, California, where she met her beloved Buffalo Billy.

She currently resides in Grass Valley and has formed a 501(c)3 nonprofit, **Buffalo Billy's Bison Brotherhood.** Her goal is to acquire ranch land for a conservation bison herd with a 5,900 sq ft lodge/headquarters. Please contact her to contribute to this endeavor for the education, protection, and promotion of our national mammal, the American Bison.

Phone/text: 925-766-1821
Email: buffalobillysbisonbrotherhood@aol.com
　　　 Myloveaffairwithbuffalobilly@aol.com

## Chapter 1

# My Love Affair
# With Buffalo Billy

### Billy's Auntie

*"Never, never be afraid to do what's right, especially
if the well-being of a person or animal is at stake.
Society's punishments are small compared
to the wounds we inflict on our soul when
we look the other way."*

~ Martin Luther King, Jr.

"**H**ow in the world did you fall in love with a buffalo?"
I've been asked that question hundreds of times
by incredulous friends and strangers. I still have
no clear answer, except to say that the buffalo was a passion
God put in my heart years before I met Buffalo Billy . . . the
1,000 lb., scruffy, humpbacked, horned, wild creature that
stole my heart and changed my life like nothing on earth
had ever done. My friends were completely baffled since
they knew me as a San Francisco Bay area-based interior
designer, obsessed with all things fine and lovely. Honestly,
I am baffled too, as buffalo, theoretically, should have been
a last pick for my life's passion. But then, I have learned that
God has a great sense of humor.

Anyone who knew me could never picture me, in what would become, my daily "buffalo uniform" of manure-stained boots, tattered jeans that even Goodwill would not accept, sweat-soaked blonde hair smashed flat under a worn-out cowboy hat, and even worse . . . sans make up! It must have been comical to watch me grinning from ear-to-ear in delight, while tending to Billy's every grungy need, in my new grungy couture.

I was, however, always wearing red lipstick because I loved making red lipstick kiss marks on Billy's crusty brown nose. Although he never actually saw them, he loved the kisses.

When I first discovered Billy, his mate, and their baby, they were skeleton-thin, suffering from what several vets guessed was malnutrition and parasites. I knew about the tragedy of the Great Bison Slaughter where, within a decade in the late 1800s, 30 to 60 million buffalo that had roamed North America for 10,000 years, were hunted nearly to extinction. While I could do nothing about that painful, historic carnage, I could do something to try to save these three, who were located just 15 minutes away from my home in Grass Valley, California.

After visiting Billy and his family every day for a week, and seeing their hopeless situation, I promised Billy I would bring them back to health. It became my sole mission, and ultimate pleasure, for the next four months.

My impossible dream had always been to have a relationship with a male bison—where I would be allowed to get close, hand feed, and actually touch him. Billy was that rare wild animal who allows you into its world and also wants to be a part of yours. It was Billy who approached me to begin what was a beautiful, trusting, and faithful love affair. I never imposed any demands on him. He set the terms and I never challenged him. And even though he had me wrapped around his hoof, he never took advantage. Rather, he responded with the same giving, caring, understanding, and acceptance that I gave to him.

Let me explain . . . Billy would come when I called him. However, buffalo only do something after they have thought about it for a while. Nothing is hurried and so I had to learn P A T I E N C E . . . a virtue I had always lacked.

My buffalo boy wanted only to be hand-fed out of a bison-sized plastic plate . . . none of this eating off-the-ground stuff for him. Holding up that plate while his 200-lb. head dined from it eliminated any further need for me to work out at the gym.

Billy would follow me around the pasture and barn as I did his housekeeping/watering duties. One day a passerby yelled from his truck, "That's a pretty big dog you have there. Nobody's going to mess with you!"

Every day Billy would be waiting for me at the fence. He would hold up his nose for the red lipstick kiss. I was allowed to pat his cheeks, but touching his sacred horns was strictly off-limits. I enjoyed learning the rules and following them.

After I finished feeding all of the animals. I would sit down on the ground at the fence and talk to Billy. He stood and listened intently and sometimes he would lie down next to me. Buffalo in a herd are constantly jabbering to each other and he loved to listen to me jabber away, as if I were just one of the herd.

Billy loved carrots and apples. Of course, he wanted them to be sliced. He liked his apples cored and expected to be handfed. He knew just how to train me, and I loved every training session.

I remember a time when my fingers were ill-placed while giving him an apple slice, and they got stuck in his mouth. I panicked and expected a sharp bite. He felt my fingers with his tongue and then looked at me intently. He pushed my fingers over to the side of his mouth with his big gnarly tongue so I could get my fingers out, and then he proceeded to eat. I was so amazed that I still had five good fingers, but he didn't seem fazed at all. It was just the thing to do . . . to look out for your Auntie.

When I think of all the amazing things Billy did, I could fill volumes. But perhaps the most amazing moments were when we would be next to each other, and he would feel the "call of nature." He would move about 25 feet away from me and relieve himself. How did he know I would not like him to poop or pee next to me? Buffalo do it next to each other all the time! To have a wild animal walk away from you, do their duty, and come back is beyond comprehension. But then, that was my Billy.

Now and again we might have a slight misunderstanding. Or better said, I wouldn't understand him. If I would do something Billy did not like, he would not hesitate to show it by giving me "The Horn." This expression is done by lowering the head and then quickly raising it, leading with one horn up. I always had to be ultra-vigilant as to where I was in proximity to him, as "The Horn" motion would not cause much more damage than a scrape to another buffalo's tough hide, but it could be fatal to a human.

On one occasion, Billy had woken up on the wrong side of the barn and was in an ornery mood. I wasn't paying as much attention to him as he wanted and he gave me "The Mock Charge," which is a more serious warning than "The Horn." That is where a bison lifts up both front feet and lunges forward, sometimes including "The Horn" maneuver. It's like having an SUV suddenly lunging toward you, only with the added terror of sharp horns attached. The problem with "The Mock Charge" is that you don't know if it is a "mock" or a full-on charge.

The Level 3 Warning is the most serious and means a charge is on the way; the bison is really angry and wants to do something about it. This is the "Raised Tail." If you see a tail raising, you are in serious trouble and need to back off if you can. Fortunately, the only time I saw tails rising was when the bison smelled a coyote. I saw the tails go up and I looked in the direction they were looking but saw nothing initially. Later, I caught a glimpse of the coyote. A bison's eyesight isn't great, but their noses pick up scents long before we can see things.

Bison are, and always will be, wild animals. They can be tamed to a point but cannot be domesticated. They must be dealt with carefully and cautiously at all times. That respect and understanding kept me safe.

After four months of supervision and treatment from the local vet, and with help from a bison expert from the University of Saskatchewan, "The Kids" (Billy's mate and baby) were putting on weight and looking better but Billy was lagging behind. They had received a wider variety of food, and more tests (that we were able to take without proper handling facilities) but Billy still wasn't responding. He was getting worse. I called the vet again on that last night. My heart broke in two as I realized Billy was dying. I just couldn't process that. Billy dying was never an option. I had promised Billy he would get well. This just could not happen.

The vet made a last-ditch effort with antibiotics because we did not know at the time exactly what was wrong. We didn't know then that Billy had been a hopeless case from the beginning. The parasites had done too much damage. He had slowly starved to death. What made the terrible tragedy worse is that no animal should die such a horrible death from common parasites. All they need is an over-the-counter dose of dewormer.

The next morning I rushed to the barn and Billy was down. He looked so pitiful and seemed almost embarrassed. I struggled to get his huge head up on a bale of hay so he would not suffocate. I spoke to him softly and stroked his beautiful face. He gave me his total trust. I gave him my all. There I was, being as close to him as I had never dreamed was possible. There was no barrier between us . . . nothing physical, nothing human or wild, no limitations of fear or hesitation of motive. It was a complete understanding of each other—a total surrender to nothing but love.

We filled giant-size syringes with electrolytes and Billy let me squirt them down his throat. He stuck his tongue out for me to give him his favorite apples. I begged him to hold on. We had called the fire department to come help get him up.

That last hour of his life was the best hour of my life, as well as the most painful and traumatic. There was nothing else I could do for him and nothing more I could give him to help him. He looked up at me with such knowing, love, and peace. It was just he and I, in our little love affair, and me jabbering to keep him alive.

The firemen came, animal control came, and so did the vet. The only thing that didn't come was a miracle. Billy died as peacefully and heroically as he had lived. Before he died, I thanked him for everything he gave me and taught me. I told him we would be together again. I told him I would forever be sorry that I had made a promise to him that was not mine to give.

*I miss you, Billy.*

## Author's Notes:

Please read the complete book, *My Love Affair with Buffalo Billy*, which is sold on Amazon, or wherever books are sold. You will discover much more about bison, Buffalo Billy, and his Auntie, and what happened to Billy's mate and baby. Profits from the book go to fund Buffalo Billy's Bison Brotherhood.

Buffalo Billy's Bison Brotherhood is a 501(c)3 non-profit organization that was formed to honor Billy and all bison that have suffered abuse or neglect at the hands of man. The Brotherhood is the only organization that targets bison rescue, and advocates in all ways for the care and protection of our national mammal, the American Bison.

The current focus of The Brotherhood is to acquire ranch land for a bison herd to roam in perpetuity and to build a 5,900 square foot lodge/headquarters with an initial capacity of 16 guests.

The plan for the ranch and lodge is to:

- Maintain, in perpetuity, a healthy and free-roaming conservation herd in as natural a way as possible.

- Allow the public to safely experience the thrill of observing bison in a natural habitat.

- Have events, programs, and entertainment venues that promote bison and agricultural education and preservation,

- Develop and provide a model for prospective or current bison ranchers to maintain a herd through profitable means, other than raising them for meat.

- Donate guestrooms and meeting spaces periodically to organizations whose programs would directly benefit from interaction with bison and nature.

- Participate in non-invasive, humane bison research because so little is known about bison specifically.

Donations of land, equipment, building materials, labor, and money are greatly appreciated to reach our goal. Please contact Billy's Auntie by phone or text at 925-766-1821.

*"But ask the animals and
they will teach you . . ."*

~ Job 12:7

**Christy Gurley** is a multidisciplinary artist from California, USA, with multiple forms of synesthesia. She has always had a special relationship with the arts, including painting, drawing, and dance. She is fascinated with languages, traveling, and culture. Christy has degrees in International Relations and Biological Sciences and did humanitarian work in east and south Africa and the Bahamas.

Christy has been creating art professionally since 1999 and her creations on canvas, paper, and original clothing can be found globally.

Since finding out that synesthesia is a phenomenon, her goal has been to increase recognition of synesthesia among children, families, and in educational settings. Christy's latest project is a series of early children's books about synesthesia, each with a story featuring a child from a different country and a different form of Synesthesia. The first book is called, *Sereya's Superpower* and is available on Amazon.

**Website: StarshineDesignsArt.com**

**Chapter 2**

# Being Yourself Is Your Real Superpower:
## *Adventures in Synesthesia*
### Christy Gurley

*"Beauty begins the moment*
*you decide to be yourself."*
~ Coco Chanel

Artistic ideas and projects brimming with color, scent, taste, and texture run through my head often as I go through my everyday life, and my art and designs are the way I capture them. The experience of walking in a park, or through a field of flowers, can be like a mini-vacation to me. I can taste the bright colors of the flower petals on my tongue, and "see" the chirp of the birds with what I can most closely describe as something like an extra layer of color and texture on top. I can feel the texture of the grass and rocks on my fingers just by looking at them and feel the temperature and movement of the cool bubbling water of the creek on my skin, with a light sense of drinking the water when I look at the creek. Listening to my favorite music on my walk, there are bursts of colors, sounds, and shapes as each instrument plays. The voices of some singers have their own color, and some genres of music have patterns and movement.

This is just a normal part of my world and always has been. Can you imagine what it was like for me to hear, for the first time, that other people don't experience these things? I honestly didn't believe it. It's probably a lot like what you are thinking now if you are reading about these things for the first time.

How could those brightly colored petals not give you a taste like gummy bears? Your warm purple isn't majestic, haughty, and fuzzy like velvet? I would think you were playing a joke on me.

This phenomenon has a name: it's called *synesthesia*, a neurological trait that is found in some form in around 4% of people around the world. It causes people (called *synesthetes*) to experience sensory input/response by two different unrelated senses at the same time. Examples include: seeing shapes when hearing sounds; visualizing colors, genders, and personalities when seeing letters and numbers; and experiencing shapes and colors when eating. Any two senses can mix together, and synesthesia is involuntary. I can't choose what a word tastes like or change a piano's color from a warm palette to a cool one.

Many people with synesthesia are highly creative and go into the arts. They often do not find out they are different from other people until later in life because they don't realize that they see the world any differently than anyone else. In fact, most synesthetes love having synesthesia and would definitely not give it up. It brings an extra sort of magic to their world. Although documented for over 100 years, it is just recently that synesthesia is slowly becoming more known. Now there is information about it online and you can find books ranging from children's stories (like mine) to college-level texts.

It tends to be in school where synesthetes discover that they view things a little differently. Unfortunately, if they mention that the color of the pen used on the whiteboard is "too loud", or that the sound from next door is "causing too much interference from the colors or shapes," they might be scolded, or sent to the principal's office, or made fun of by the other kids.

It's important to know that if a student reads a little more slowly because the letter "o" and the letter "u" don't get along, they aren't making this up—it's simply a part of the way their brain works. (The type of synesthesia where letters and numbers have personalities is called "Ordinal Linguistic Personification".)

There are over 80 different recorded forms of synesthesia, and it has been definitively confirmed with brain scans. It is currently considered part of the neurodiversity spectrum but is hard to classify in the current educational system because it is more of an additional, or bonus, sense. Unless they are already familiar with it, teachers might not have current information or even believe it is a real phenomenon.

I am a "polysynesthete," which means someone with multiple forms of synesthesia. I've had it my whole life, I just never knew synesthesia 'existed' until a few years ago when I saw a passing reference in a newspaper article about someone seeing colors when they heard music. I thought, *Why would they think this is newsworthy?* But it stuck in my head. After a week or so, I started researching more about it and what I found out absolutely changed my world.

Were they actually saying that people didn't see colors when they heard music? That blue didn't have a personality? That they couldn't feel the scrape on their skin when someone else tripped and fell? No way. I didn't believe it!

Thank goodness for that newspaper story. I started finding out everything I could about synesthesia and its many different forms. How could I have two science degrees and have never heard of this? To me, my experiences were as normal as breathing, but I still had never met anyone who said they had it.

For a long time, I thought everyone experienced the same things I did. It still surprises me when I find out someone else doesn't experience life the way I do, and I suspect that I will be learning about those differences for a lifetime. As for me, I'm happy with the way my colors feel, the delectable tastes of the luminous light streaming through leaves and stained glass, and the dance of color, shades, and textures when I hear music. Now that I know my experiences are unique I actually enjoy them even more. It's something I often refer to as my "Candy Land world." I wouldn't give it up for anything.

I know I am one of the lucky ones—some synesthetes can be overwhelmed by the ways their synesthesia affects them. I still haven't met any who would opt out of having it though.

I was a dancer for many years of my life. I always knew I had a special relationship with music. I never counted notes the way others did; the music was a language unto itself and dance was a physical expression of its conversation. I could feel the expression of the music in every part of myself. It had colors, movement, flavor, and texture. I would say, "Isn't this song beautiful?" and people would agree. But I never knew that we weren't talking about the same thing! I never had any reason to question it—and neither did they. I wish I knew then what I know now. Sometimes I imagine where life could have taken me, but things often come to you at the right time. So now, I imagine where my life will go in the future.

Nowadays, I am a very prolific artist. But like many, I had a long period of an artistic block— or what I can more accurately call an absolute creative wasteland. For about eight years, I simply could not make any form of artwork that expressed what I wanted to convey; I couldn't draw things as I saw them in my head. Looking back, I think I started to compare myself with other artists and lost my own vision.

My art has generally been quite different than other people's. I painted mostly abstracts and I would listen to the music and paint what I felt and saw in front of me. I'd sit blissfully ensconced in the music with colors, movements, patterns, emotions, and sometimes temperatures, that came along with whatever I was listening to. Sometimes I would just go outside and envelop myself in the sounds, the colors, and the feeling of the breeze on my skin. All of this is what I painted. It wasn't everybody's reality or artistic vision, but it was mine, and my art was just for me.

I didn't even intend to become an artist—I worked with animals in zoos, and in labs with microscopes and test tubes. In fact, I typically threw my artwork away and it was only when people started pulling my paintings out of the trash and asking to buy them that I became a professional artist!

During the years I wasn't painting, I took up other hobbies and volunteer work. I was able to help with great causes, learn new things, and meet people from all around the world. I wouldn't trade those experiences for anything but I wondered if I was ever going to get my artistic verve back.

Then came Covid, and everyone else took a hiatus, too. For me, it was great. I'm a researcher at heart and I read and watched everything I could find about these cool things I experienced that apparently few others did! As a matter of fact, there were so few, that I had still never met a single person I could talk to about it.

During that time, I found online synesthesia chats and other groups. Although none of us experienced our synesthesia in exactly the same way, we understood each other in a way no one else did. Having the opportunity to virtually attend Zoom conferences with other synesthetes was a thrill, and I wanted more than anything to meet these people in the real world and find out more.

I learned that there was an international conference on synesthesia coming up. Although I didn't know a soul where it was being held, or how I was going to get there, I decided that I was going! Until my dying day, I will probably consider this the best thing I've ever done—it was like the world opened up.

Being with other "Synnies," who could explain the ways they lived with this phenomenon, was so freeing. I wanted to hear every story, every experience, every example of how people experienced their synesthesia. Talking with them also helped me discover I had other forms of synesthesia that I hadn't realized existed. (To date, I have identified around 10 forms, in various strengths.) Most people were very good at describing their experiences, which helped me a lot because I am still learning to put those things into words. Some of these synesthetes experience their forms in ways that blow my mind, and I love to listen to all of it! I felt the most intense kinship with every one of the synesthetes who attended the conference—like we were some kind of twins.

But the flip side of that wonderful coin was finding out about their own experiences in school and while growing up. Many went through things that ranged from disappointing to horrifying. The majority had been made fun of in school because they were "different." If they talked about what they saw when reading, writing, or learning in school, many teachers would accuse them of trying to get attention or of disrupting the class. They would get in trouble for simply being themselves; hampering their learning and teaching them that they had to keep their reality a secret.

I was stunned and truly disturbed to discover that decades ago when people weren't as open or knowledgeable about neurodiversity, kids were threatened with being forcibly institutionalized or were given strong medications to "turn off" their synesthesia. This absolutely broke my heart. Not only did I hurt for what they'd been through, but I realized how incredibly lucky I have been. I've always marched to the beat of my own drum and don't know how I would have reacted if people had made fun of me, or teachers had gotten after me, for things that were genuinely normal parts of my brain and learning type.

After hearing so many people's awful experiences, I realized that more people need to know about synesthesia and understand what it is. After all, I've had it my whole life, and I didn't know anything about it either. I was moved to start writing books for children to help them identify and be excited about the special innate gifts they have. I felt it was important to make these books for the parents and grandparents too, so they could learn about and support these gifts in their children and grandchildren.

It has been very rewarding to hear that this has already had an effect on children and families who have read my first children's story, *Sereya's Superpower*, about experiencing synesthesia. I heard from one mother who, after reading the book to her children, told me they both said, "Mommy, we want to have that superpower, too!" Just from hearing the story in a different light, her children were accepting something different as being "cool." I was thrilled to imagine that putting these books out into the world would be beneficial to those with, and without synesthesia.

One of my goals is to make synesthesia more well-known and accepted in the educational arena, so that teachers are able to recognize that what the children are experiencing is not a cry for attention—it is simply a normal part of their existence. I'm a strong believer that kids need to be brought up with love and self-confidence, so they can feel secure in their own skins. This is something everyone deserves.

I also learned that synesthesia is much better known in some countries than in others. I feel that a good way to have the most people identify with this information is to talk about synesthesia through the eyes of different children from around the world; each story will feature a little girl or boy with a different form. My first book was a bit of an autobiography and talks about several forms I have and how I experience them.

My goal is to help spread the word wherever I can so that parents, grandparents, and teachers find out what synesthesia is and recognize it as special when they come across these unique and wonderful individuals. So I am releasing *Sereya's Superpower* in multiple languages. So far it has been translated from the original English into German, Korean, and Spanish, and I hope to have it available in many more languages in the future.

Are there other reasons to have synesthesia identified early in children? Yes! Identifying it early in life can help students develop their unique skills, improve their study techniques, and even skew their education towards careers where their synesthesia can be an extra bonus.

Some synesthetes have the most amazing careers that have come about because of their special sensory abilities. For example, some work for perfumeries to help them develop unique scents. Others work for makeup companies to help develop special colors. It's not uncommon to employ a synesthete to help create different spirits like wine or whiskey. Many synesthetes find their way into the arts— whether it be painting, illustrating, music, design, etc.

It has been almost a year now since I got back from the conference, and since then my life has changed immeasurably. I've begun focusing more on my unique forms of synesthesia, have given talks about it, and shared all kinds of information and resources with numerous parents and grandparents. I'm over the moon when they tell me that their kids feel like "Superstars" now, instead of outcasts, and their friends now think they have special gifts—even "Superpowers."

Best of all, I blew the top off of my artistic block. I have not stopped painting and drawing since I returned! Look for future books in my series of "Synesthesia Kids" on Amazon, and in libraries and bookstores.

*"Synesthesia is like dancing with your senses.
It's a gift I feel blessed to have and
I wouldn't give it up for the world."*

~ Christy Gurley

Music is the reason **LeRena Major** chooses to breathe. As Rena the Rockhistorygal, she's a Popular Music Memoirist and Walking Popular Music Historian who blasts her awesome, unparalleled knowledge of music history into the world, enriching the lives of others by utilizing music as a way to cope, heal, laugh, and live. An advocate for creators, she honors and upholds the legacies of those who forge/d the soundtracks of our lives, passionately challenging damaging, systemic, and societally programmed ideals along the way.

A few of the upcoming projects from Rena's music-obsessed brain include these (and many other) works in her ongoing Music Geek Memoirs collection: *Myopia Won't Stop the Music: Thriving with Severe Myopia After Retinal Detachment*; *I'll Carry Your Casket: A Walking Popular Music Historian's Lifelong Obsession with the Deaths of Her Musical Heroes*; and *Through the Eyes of My 45's, Vol. 1*.

Supplemental material on this chapter, a Spotify playlist that sound-tracked the writing of it, and context behind the song choices can be found on Rena's website.

**Website: rockhistorygal.com**
**LinkedIn: in/lerena-major-012a5b7/**
**Email: rockhistorygal@proton.me**

## Chapter 3

# Third Quarter
## *(Or . . . I Know What It Feels Like)*
### LeRena Major

*"Caring for myself is not self-indulgence; it is self-preservation, and that is an act of political warfare."*
~ Audre Lorde

**M**usic is the reason why I continue to exist. Music has never let me down, though people often have.

I've spent basically my entire life—since just before the age of five—acquiring Questlove-level knowledge about the people, places, things, legalities, and much more about the very wide world of popular music. My knowledge spans from Edison's invention of the phonograph to the present day. I evangelize about popular music history to anyone who'll listen.

Without music, there's no Rena. It's my air, my fuel, and my everything. I love to talk to people—and I love to talk about popular music history. Gifted with synesthesia, I see music and syllables in patterns—and in sheet music—in front of me. I think in multiple languages.

When I turned 50, almost two years ago, I entered what I call my Third Quarter: literally my third quarter-century of life. 2024 marks my 35th year in the workforce. Unashamed to reveal my age, I do so happily, as I've had to fight and claw for every moment, just like so many women all over the world. Hiding my age won't combat sexism. Instead, I proudly, vibrantly flaunt it so the world can see that I'm not past some imaginary human sell-by date.

I definitely plan to make my Third Quarter count. I'll share more on that after we press "Rewind" on my life just a little bit.

I'd like you to take a moment, badass reader, and think about hardship and trauma in your life, and then say to yourself, out loud, "I know what it feels like to. . ." finishing off your words by verbalizing your experiences of adversity.

I am here as your ally and support system. I know what it feels like.

I know what it feels like to have a racist, sexist, homophobic, physically abusive mother. She hit me for years to express her displeasure that I didn't share her horrible, disgusting belief system. I grew up in a rural, economically depressed area of Central Pennsylvania, and I knew then no one would believe me. It's difficult to get taken seriously now as many people tend to instantly sympathize with parents. I continue to work to normalize the fact that it's never okay to glamorize or defend abusive parents.

I know what it feels like to have that mother try to smash my head into an old-school metal radiator (of which there were several in our old home). I thought, "Hell, no" (actually, some much spicier words went through my head, but I'll save them for the edgier, NSFW version of this story) and I fought back—hard. Infuriated, she retaliated by trying to throw me down the cellar stairs. I stretched my arms out as far as I could in the doorway at the top of the stairs and held firm—in the same way I scrunched my feet in my sneakers to keep the school bully from stepping on the backs of them to pull them off—and I somehow emerged the victor. I don't know how I would have explained my injuries at school if she had succeeded. I also know that I may not be alive if she had.

I know what it feels like to have that mother force you to stand in front of the coal furnace that my father installed in the cellar and burn the records with which she caught me—and make me inhale the toxic fumes—because she disliked secular music. My father would help me get the records—only to have her take them away from me.

I know what it feels like to have a racist, homophobic, verbally abusive father pin you to the wall at your workplace in front of coworkers, yelling and screaming at you for no fault of your own, then leave after handing you a bag of fast food. I saw him punch lots of doors and walls. My parents were both manipulative, each trying to pit me against the other, while still being physically and verbally abusive. It was a massively f*cked up way to grow up. Nobody else knew as I hid it from the outside world.

I know what it feels like to go through menopause and have multiple medical professionals tell me I was too young and that I must have been lying about the date of my last menstrual period. It was pure gaslighting. I have no reason to lie about anything, let alone this. As all who menstruate (or used to) know, it's a once-a-month quality of life reduction that frequently arrives more than once a month. I've been beyond thrilled to be rid of it, despite the accompanying symptoms. Postmenopausal for several years, I continue to work to normalize talking about it as much as possible.

I know what it feels like to be told by some of these same medical professionals that I shouldn't have my tubes tied since I'll want to have a baby with a man. It was, and still is, a massively inappropriate thing to say and is no basis to deny care. I'm a person, not a baby-making machine. Plenty of people do awesome things and never reproduce, never having the desire to do so. I am one of them. I will fight the heteronormative patriarchy that still runs society until I take my last breath.

I know what it's like to be told, many times over the years, that I can't possibly be busy for the end-of-year holiday season—or be so good at any of the things I do— since I (purposefully) never had children.

I know what it's like to be my usual, positive, cheerful, hardworking, respectful, assertive self in the workplace and be told to dial it down. The men telling me I was overbearing were, and still are, celebrated for the same traits.

I know what it's like to have a male coworker tell me directly to my face, on the workplace floor in front of other employees, that higher wages should only go to people like him who have mortgages and children. He said I don't deserve to make a higher wage since I don't have to pay for those things. I verbally ripped him apart (professionally, of course, but quite firmly) in front of everyone watching.

They knew I meant business. Do you have any idea what happened to that man after that? Yep, you guessed it: he got promoted.

I know what it's like to have a male coworker grab you by the arm, drag you to a slightly more remote area of the workplace floor, and yell at you—mad because a project was moved off his plate and onto yours. I cautioned the executive who made that decision against this because of just such a result. Told I must be overreacting, that executive then gaslighted me. The Human Resources Manager did the same. Such behavior is so rampant in workplaces and society because people in power allow it to happen. I've never once seen that fancy policy called "zero tolerance" be truly enforced.

I know what it feels like to propose great ideas in the workplace, only to be shot down by male executives. When a male coworker proposes the same idea later in the day, it's celebrated. When proposing a much-needed role within the organization, I was told that the role wasn't needed. What happened next may not surprise you: a male coworker learned of my idea, proposed it to the same executive—and was granted the role. I've been gaslighted so many times in my career with the "we really need you in your current role since you're so good at what you do" line as an excuse to deny your advancement.

I know what it's like to attempt to calculate all the wages I've lost, during my lengthy career, due to what's between my legs. Even with the mostly low-wage jobs I have steadfastly worked (plus a couple of short-lived stints at modestly paid roles as the creative path I walk doesn't usually lead to monetary abundance but still requires a massive amount of hard work), my head still spins at the amount of money the system has taken from me and millions of others due to income inequality—and I'm white! It's even worse for women of color.

I know what it feels like to live for many years in what most would call the poorer areas of the city and be a minority in those spaces. I've witnessed shootings, stabbings, and other crimes—because I was literally not paid enough to afford to live anywhere else, no matter how hard I worked or how highly I was educated.

I know what it feels like to be a beautiful, sexually fluid woman who does not—and never has and proudly never will—fit any kind of conventional beauty norm. This has brought me steady scrutiny, criticism—and jealousy—because I get dates, physical pleasure, and other enjoyable things in life because my confidence is attractive. I have never been a thin woman, and although I have experienced a life-altering weight loss recently, I am not thin, nor do I want to be. Society, though, still looks at me as the third wheel and has massive difficulty accepting that I love myself and have significant confidence in what I do and how I look. Some perceive me as a threat. I am no one's third wheel, I'll tell you that.

I know what it feels like to be in an interracial marriage and be denied housing—at the turn of the last century and three-plus decades after *Loving v. Virginia*. We were told to our faces that the landlord didn't want to rent to people like us. I most certainly put forth a fiery, verbal protest at this treatment.

I know what it feels like to watch your black ex-spouse be harassed by police for driving while black, sitting in a car while black, and yes, existing while black. I had a front-row seat, and I was most certainly appalled by what I saw. This was many years before Black Lives Matter, since this treatment of blacks and other people of color is in no way new. I live in a country that was founded on racism, sexism, inequality, theft, and freedom for only some. I shouldn't even have to be writing any of this. We still have such a long way to go.

I know what it's like to watch my former father-in-law, a transgender woman and legendary elder in the community, who was present at Stonewall and has fought her whole life for transgender rights, experience transphobia when others realize that we were not kidding when introducing her: "She's my father-in-law." Many times, I was told that I had made a mistake and must have meant my mother-in-law. No, my mother-in-law is a completely different person. You could see the hatred across many faces. A front-row seat to transphobia or any kind of injustice is never a good experience—it's sickening—and I will continue to fight fiercely for equality for all.

I know what it's like to watch my ex-spouse descend into cocaine addiction—which had nothing to do with me—and almost destroy my life by stealing from me. Many nights I slept with my ID, debit card, and old flip phone in my pillowcase with the phone cord trailing out into the wall socket so I could protect what little I had.

I know what it's like to rise from the ashes of that whole situation, working seven days a week for years at low-wage jobs to survive and put myself on a course for a happier future. It certainly wasn't the first time I had worked seven days a week at low-wage jobs to survive.

I know what it's like to experience food insecurity across multiple stages of my life. I plan to be an activist in this area in the future.

I know what it feels like to think I'm the poster child for the concept that years and years of incredibly hard work don't get you very far. Real life just doesn't seem to work like that for most of us. Then I realized that I was one of the many, many millions of pixels on the poster.

I know what it feels like to be told repeatedly during my life—from my childhood to the present in my sixth decade of life—that I can't do something that I want to do and that I have to change myself in order to succeed. I've been underestimated my whole damn life.

I need more than the digits on both of my hands to count the times during my life and career that these kinds of things have happened to me. I'm not perfect, but I'm not the problem. I pride myself on always being the hardest worker in the room who's always willing to do what needs to be done, training and helping others so that they can thrive. I am fun, funny, make friends easily, and don't do drama. I am confident and assertive in how I carry myself. I don't seek or need anyone's validation. These things are still considered a threat by so many. I know I am not alone in these experiences, not by a long shot, and it paints a vivid picture of what it's still like to exist on this planet as a woman.

I don't want to hear you say you're sorry that all of these things happened to me. I want to hear you say *that you wish they wouldn't have happened and take action in helping to combat such unthinkable behavior.* Help me try to change one mind at a time, even if it's just talking to others whenever you can about how wrong these things are. I bristle when people say they're sorry to me. "Sorry" is an escape route: "It wasn't me, so I can now slink away and wipe my hands of this information." Personal experience with a topic is not required for you to be an empathetic supporter and an ally for change.

It doesn't always have to be this way. I also know what it's like in my current job to never once experience sexism, toxicity, or microaggressions—for more than two years. I'm so proud of my team for that and have ensured that they and my supervisor know.

I think forward and outward, not up. There's no ceiling, let alone a glass one. I believe that thinking about being above people or climbing a ladder only strengthens inequality. I will continue to speak up where others won't— or can't.

*Now, let's get back to the music, shall we?*

Music has gotten me through all of this and more. I latched onto it during the mid-70s with 8-tracks, cassettes, vinyl, and the radio (all of which I still use, plus streaming, and more!) and I found my salvation. It's been the main thread on which my entire life's been woven.

My paternal grandmother was my namesake—a woman of French ancestry named Rena Elizabeth Billotte. I call her "The Original Rena" (great documentary name, I know.) My father frequently mentioned that she was musical, and I suspect I take after her. She never got to see her Third Quarter—the part of my life that I am navigating now because she died at age 35—18 years before I was born—and when my father, who would now be 85 if he were alive, was 15.

I have no idea if I will get a Fourth Quarter, so I'm making this one count. I'd like to make that documentary after researching her life more, living as fearlessly as possible as I do it, and imagining what she would've done with the years she didn't get—her Third Quarter. I also plan to explore my mother's Slovak and English ancestry plus Rena's marriage to a man of Irish descent.

I'll continue to live my life boldly, openly, loudly, and confidently. I am the change that I want to see in the world. Dancing like no one is watching is an everyday occurrence for me —as is singing out loud in the grocery store! I am somehow quite sure "The Original Rena" would approve.

I have so much to do in my Third Quarter (and beyond!) including what is my life's work: sharing a never-ending series of memoirs (including poems!) told through the lens of music, keeping my musical heroes visible and vibrant while also working at the crucial intersection of music and mental health. This includes a book on how tumultuous and transformative my last year has been, dealing with surgery due to complications of an inherited vision condition that will threaten my livelihood for the rest of my life. I am living proof that all these experiences will not stop me from thriving and being happy.

You don't stand out from the pack by doing what the pack does. I live by that example. I'm literally spending the rest of my life celebrating and upholding the legacies of those who create the soundtracks of our lives so that I can also help people cope, heal, laugh, and live - with music.

I'm proud to be a contributor to *The Cinderella Monologues, Volume 2* with this awe-inspiring assembly of women. I almost didn't participate as I was initially turned off by the name of the book. Don't be fooled, though, by the typical renderings of the Cinderella story. If you dig deeper into the origins of the folk tale, it's really about women overcoming adversity on their own terms.

Yeah, I know a little something about that.

**Gale Pylman** is a certified aromatherapist and enjoys teaching others about the world of essential oils, among her many class offerings. She has always nurtured a relationship with herbs and flowers, having grown up gardening with her mom in a small town in Northern California.

While earning her B.S. degree in Horticulture at CSU, Chico, she learned various aspects of landscape plants, but nothing can replace the delight she feels when out in her own garden. This background made it easier for her to become an aromatherapist, working with essential oils that are plants distilled from all over the world, and has helped her connect with nature on an entirely different level.

Researching and developing personal body care and home care recipes, and teaching others this ancient craft, has been a new path for Gale. Seeing the successes of her students has made it very enjoyable!

**Website: AngelsAndAlchemy.net**

## Chapter 4

# Always Looking
# For the Silver Lining

### Gale Pylman

*"The capacity to learn is a gift;*
*The ability to learn is a skill;*
*The willingness to learn is a choice."*
~ Brian Herbert

My mom always said I was so lucky that if I fell in the river I wouldn't get wet! But my luck ran out in 2003.

My dad died, and I think he was my lucky charm. Two weeks later, on my daughter's 13th birthday, I took a tumble and broke my ankle. No big deal for most people. But, while I was in the hospital, the IV drip monitoring my morphine broke and flooded my body, giving me an overdose. This happened during a staff shift change, so no nurses were monitoring me. My girlfriend, Maxine, came to visit and found me not breathing, with no heartbeat, and my skin was blue. She alerted the nurses, who pumped me full of Narcan and brought me back to life.

I don't have a recollection of that event, and if Maxine hadn't told me about the incident, I wouldn't have ever known. It wasn't written in my chart and they never mentioned it to me or my husband, Jeff.

Everyone asks me what having a Near Death Experience (NDE) was like. The time frame itself was unremarkable, and the last thing I remember was bragging to my husband, when he visited that morning, that I was so proud I hadn't needed to press my pain-relief IV button to release any morphine into my system. I must be healing at a really fast rate! It took almost a year before things 'changed' and my health started to get much worse.

I had a checkup with my regular MD several months later and mentioned I was having problems forming sentences. Words seemed just out of reach but felt like they were on the tip of my tongue. I felt more tired and didn't feel refreshed after a night's sleep. A silver lining turned out to be that my husband and I laughed when I had to pantomime my thoughts, as I couldn't remember the words I wanted to say!

My MD basically said I had been working too hard and I should take some time off. He didn't offer any testing, or to further explore how the overdose of morphine might have affected me. And yes, I *was* working harder. Taking time off? Not an option. I had a bookkeeping business and needed to meet payroll and other tax deadlines for my clients. Our daughter had been diagnosed with autism, and since my husband worked 50 miles from home, I was the one tasked with helping her by setting up Individualized Education Program (IEP) meetings and researching everything I could find on autism. Plus, my mom needed a lot of support and help after my dad had passed.

One day, I decided that I absolutely couldn't make it out to see my clients. I stayed in bed—and wasn't able to get up for over a year; I was way beyond bone-tired. My body stopped speaking to me and I didn't know why. I felt a lot of pain all over my body, especially in my back and on the outsides of my thighs. Even running water from the shower hurt. I am a voracious reader, but I couldn't hold up a book, or concentrate enough to read, or even watch T.V. I was so tired, I couldn't even cry. My emotions had switched off. I could barely feed myself, yet I started gaining weight.

My persistence with the doctor resulted in a diagnosis of fibromyalgia, and he said I would just have to adjust to this new modified lifestyle. Not very specific, but he gave me a lot of prescriptions! Fibromyalgia is a chronic immune disorder that is hard to pin down. The symptoms range from digestive issues and trouble sleeping, to pain sensitivity, arthritis, and brain fog. There is no known cure, and unfortunately, there are still many doctors who tell their patients, "There is nothing wrong, it's all in your head." I had a prescription for everything, *plus* meds for the side effects of the other medications.

It became very hard for my family and friends to understand what I was going through, as symptoms would flare up and cause me to be bedridden for several days. Then I would feel fine for a week before another flare-up would come on. Well-meaning friends would say I looked fine and that I couldn't possibly be sick. Why was I ghosting them and not showing up for meetings or parties? Or, they would tell me they had "a cure." I tried every one of their suggestions that contained an ounce of common sense, and several that didn't! Nothing worked or even helped. And then there was my friend who told me fibromyalgia was simply a fad, and that I wasn't really sick at all. She became my ex-friend in a hurry.

I asked my husband to divorce me, not because I didn't love him, but because I loved him so much that I didn't want him to be stuck with a wife who couldn't share a life with him. My horizon became very bleak, and that light at the end of the tunnel? I truly thought it was an oncoming train. I thought if I could get Jeff to leave me, he could marry someone who would be able to care for him the way I wanted to, and not be a burden to him. I planned to "take myself out" later, so he wouldn't have to worry about me.

His response? I still remember it so clearly. We drove to a park and walked to a nearby picnic table, surrounded by a large green lawn, with a variety of ornamental trees planted all around, close to a large pond. There, he told me he loved me; he wasn't going to leave me and to get that nonsense out of my head. He planned to stay with me for the rest of our lives, regardless of the situations we found ourselves in, and I needed to turn my thoughts around and start enjoying life with him again, even if it wasn't at all what we had hoped and dreamed of. I'm happy to say we have now been married for over 38 years.

As I struggled to get out of bed each day, I came up with a way to visually share my energy level. With—of all things—those little pink spoons you get when tasting ice cream. Can you imagine a spoon as a measurement of energy? In general terms, kids seem to have *tablespoons* of energy! They go and go and go—running, jumping, playing—all day long. Adults have *teaspoons* of energy. They live their lives going to work, spending time with family, doing chores, but don't have the same energy levels as children do. Those of us with autoimmune disorders, such as fibromyalgia, have *tiny pink tasting spoons* of energy, and they are small, and made of easily breakable plastic that isn't meant for everyday use.

Then you calculate the number of spoons per day. Let's randomly choose ten spoons per person. A child with ten tablespoons can go all day! An adult tends to use their teaspoons to get them through 12-14 hours, winding down at the end of each day. Those of us with fibro use all ten of our little pink spoonfuls before lunch.

I realized that if I was going to have a chance at getting better, Western medicine wasn't going to help me enough. So, I would make myself sit at my computer and take notes about the information I found on the internet because I couldn't remember anything once I read it. My ability to recall both short- and long-term items seemed random and definitely became worse over time.

My husband took over the household and cooked for all of us, including my mom, while working so far from home. We had a wonderful housekeeper, Margie, who kept us sanitary! My mom helped out with picking up our daughter after school and taking care of her until Jeff arrived home in the evening from work and running errands.

After another year plus my energy began to return, albeit very slowly. I had gained 90 pounds. My mind started to function better, so I was at least able to read gardening magazines. A friend gave me a book, *When Sleeping Beauty*

*Wakes Up* by Patt Lynd-Kyle. In it, she references that about 10% of those diagnosed with fibromyalgia will recover and I determined I would be included in that number!

I became so adamant that I would get better, that I started researching alternative solutions. I needed to make my soul happy again, so I started a flower garden, and located it in a sunny area on our property, about 500 feet from our house. It was exhausting for me to even get there, but once I did, I crawled on my hands and knees between the rows to weed and till the soil with a hand trowel, because to me, it felt good!

I grew all sorts of beautiful and interesting flowers: Green Bells of Ireland, Celosia with their weird sea anemone-like waves in eye-popping colors, clove-scented Sweet William, Teddy Bear and burgundy-colored sunflowers. I grew nothing I considered run-of-the-mill, because I truly thought it might be the last garden I would grow in my life, and I wanted it to be unique. I really don't have any idea how much time I spent in that garden, but I would fall asleep between the rows of sunflowers; they were tall and offered the most shade. When I would awaken I would make my way back to the house, where I showered and went back to bed.

Next, Jeff and I created a magical fairy garden much closer to the house. We still love spending time there, under the shade of "Grandmother Oak." It was at the fairy garden, that my friend, Luci, an herbalist and aromatherapist, introduced me to essential oils and I began my studies in aromatherapy.

I tried various combinations of oils and was very

impressed by the results, as they helped alleviate many of my fibromyalgia symptoms. Subsequently I started weaning myself off most of the medications my doctor had prescribed. Until then, I hadn't realized I was taking 12 different medications every day! I felt disgusted—at my doctor, who only increased the number and dosage of pills—and at myself, for allowing this to happen.

I persevered, finding more ways to incorporate essential oils on a daily basis, eating local farm-fresh foods, drinking herbal teas, and napping in my gardens. I got better! I'm still not 100%, but I'm okay with that. Now I have so much more empathy and understanding for others who have also suffered from immune disorders. *Progress, not perfection, has become my motto!*

The most amazing silver lining was that I developed psychic abilities! I seem to just "know" things about people, which are messaged to me through colors and symbols. I believe that angels give me this information to help bring a gentleness of spirit and compassion to others.

I don't often remember the readings I share, but one that stayed with me was for a former Marine. I "saw" a piece of lemon pie, and I was told he had been a young boy who had learned a lesson. That was it! Nothing more! I felt like a dummy. I didn't know what to say, so I talked about what the colors and layers of the lemon pie might represent—brown crust would represent the ground, lemon might be hot sunshine, the meringue could be a windy day . . . I found myself grasping for meaning.

The gentleman, now in his 60s, looked at me incredulously and my inner voice told me to just stop talking! I asked him if any of this made sense to him? He stared at me, then related that he grew up in Bakersfield, where every summer day is hot and windy. On one of those days, his dad took him to a bakery and bought him a piece of—you guessed it—lemon pie. As they were walking down the street, and he was enjoying his pie, they passed a stranger who was dirty, thin, and poorly dressed. His dad explained that this was a homeless man who was probably hungry. The boy felt so guilty about enjoying his lemon pie that he threw it away. He said it made such a lasting impression on him as a young boy, that to this day, he works at his church distributing food to the hungry. He then gave me a hug and thanked me for bringing this memory back into clear view again; he said he was resolved to help find a way to feed even more people. My heart was full.

I want to share what has worked for me; although I am not a doctor and can't/won't give medical advice, these common-sense items may make a positive difference in your life.

1.  **Never give up!** I now truly believe I am here on this earth for a purpose, and I believe you are, too. Life can be hard, but it is still worth the work. One of my morning mantras is: "Fall down twice, get up three times." It changes in the afternoonto : "Fall down five times, get up six! Then rest!"

2.  **Keep a sense of humor.** Lost yours? Read jokes or watch a funny movie. Figure out a way to laugh, because laughter really does help!

3.  **It's okay to feel and express emotions**. I used to never cry, or let people see me upset, mad, or sad. I was raised to always have a mask on and not show my

emotions. "Never let them see you sweat" went out the window! But it is important to remember to express your feelings towards the people who actually made you feel that way. Don't yell at your kids or dog if your girlfriend pissed you off—yell at her!

4. **Let go of a perfect lifestyle.** Life is messy—for everyone. Don't be afraid to say no to projects, committees, and chores. One of my favorite quotes is from Abraham Hicks, "Saying no to one thing means you are saying yes to something else." Be sure that what you say yes to brings you joy.

5. **Ask for help.** Oh boy, this is still a tough one for me! A friend gave me a perspective that helped me reframe this. She asked me, "How do you feel when you help someone?' I replied, "I feel good, and happy when I can be of service." "Well then," she said, "Why don't you let the rest of us feel happy and be of service to you more often?" Point taken.

6. **Take care of *you*.** I looked deeply at every aspect of my life and tried to make improvements. When a chiropractor suggested I go off gluten, I thought she was crazy. But I did it anyway, because desperate times call for desperate measures, right? It helped. Plus, I lost 20 lbs. I learned to meditate instead of yelling at the Universe. It helped. I switched to using products made from natural ingredients, eliminating as many man-made chemicals from my world as possible. I still take time to rest whenever I can.

7. **Work on forgiving yourself.** Everything isn't your fault. S&#t happens. I'm still not there but I continue to work toward this goal because I know how important it is. Any type of chronic issue—whether it is a disease, syndrome, or an issue that causes stress to you and the world around you—can be forgiven. I readily took the blame for everything, from financial difficulties (because I could no longer work) to our daughter's struggle with school, or because dinner wasn't cooked, or the laundry done. I thought I had very broad shoulders and could handle it all. I was wrong.

8. **Try everything (almost)!** Yes, there is a lot of quackery out there in the world, and you need to be careful and research thoroughly. But, just because I didn't know anything about a particular therapy or product, didn't mean it wasn't worth trying. And many of them helped me! They may or may not help you, but how will you know? To help alleviate my pain, my husband not only became a massage therapist but also a Reiki Master. I tried accupressure, accupuncture, sound healing, light therapy, hypnotherapy, along with supplements, creams, and tinctures. I have tried a lot of products, exercises, and techniques, and spent a lot of time, energy, and money, all in an effort to try and rid myself of this rotten chronic disease. I now have specific routines and supplements I take every day that help me. And the ones that didn't work? I have no regrets. I don't want to look back and say, "Wow, if only I had tried . . ."

In conclusion, please look for the silver lining. A friend turned on a light bulb in my brain recently when he said,

"What if this is the way it is supposed to look when it is all working out?" I had to spend some serious time with that thought.

It's been over 20 years since I was diagnosed with fibromyalgia, and not at all the life I ever imagined! Yet, I can still count my blessings every day. I have gotten better physically, mentally, and emotionally. My husband and I have a deeper relationship due to our sense of humor—more so than when we would gallop off in opposite directions to work every morning. I can, and do, take the time to smell the roses we planted. The pets we have rescued over the years have all known a loving, stable life filled with TLC because I was home to care for them. The list goes on . . .

I encourage you, whether or not you have a chronic disease like fibromyalgia, to look for the silver lining in your life. Count your blessings. Be of service to someone. Laugh a lot! Send positive, loving energy out to the Universe. Maybe this is the way it is supposed to look when it is all working out!

**Ms. Karla Hill** is a seasoned HR executive, career coach, and business owner committed to equipping individuals to accomplish their economic empowerment goals. She is founder of GPS Career and Business Strategies, which helps business owners and individuals transform their organizations and careers via Human Resources tools and strategies.

Karla has a bachelor's degree from City University of New York's (CUNY) Baruch College and a master's degree from Chestnut Hill College in Philadelphia. She holds senior certifications from the Society of Human Resources Management and the Human Resources Certification Institute and is certified to administer the Myers Briggs Personality and Career Direct assessment tools. She currently serves as the Deputy Director for Human Resources for the City of Philadelphia's Department of Planning and Development.

She partners with her husband to provide custom real estate services through their firm, GPS Real Estate Solutions. In her free time, Karla enjoys spending time with her husband, two sons, and mother.

**Websites:** gpsrealestatesolutions.com
gpscareerandbusinessstrategies.com

## Chapter 5

# Lessons Learned From Cinderella
### *The Journey to Maximizing Your True Career Potential*
**Karla Hill**

*"I've come to believe that each of us has a personal calling that's as unique as a fingerprint—and that the best way to succeed is to discover what you love and then find a way to offer it to others in the form of service, working hard, and also allowing the energy of the universe to lead you."*

~ Oprah Winfrey

When one thinks of fairy tales, the last place their mind might go is to their career. But, contributing to *The Cinderella Monologues* has turned that on its head for me. This opportunity has allowed me to reflect on how the story of Cinderella relates to one of my favorite topics: the world of work. While some may dismiss a passion for work as an unhealthy obsession, I genuinely believe it's a part of my design. Reflecting on my configuration as it relates to my personality, interests, skills, and values, I feel privileged to have a passion. I am reminded of the quote by Bob Snyder, "Your passion is your life's purpose seeking outward expression." It's not only my work, but it is equipping others to perform in areas that align with their design, as well. Even as an introvert, discussions about work and careers make me come alive.

Most of us know the story: a beautiful woman whose mean stepmother forced her to work as a servant in her own home. She spent her days performing chores for her horrible stepsisters, but she always envisioned a better life. By the end of the story, Cinderella becomes a princess—embodying the audacity to believe you can go beyond your present circumstances and realize your dreams. Taken at face value, or on the surface, Cinderella's journey may seem like just another fairy tale, but upon closer examination, it follows a series of steps to help you achieve your career goals.

One of the critical variables of enjoying your work is enthusiasm. About 15 years ago, I was offered a promotion to contract manager for a facilities management organization. I believed it would allow me to blend my passion for human resources with my interest in real estate. While I just described the job correctly, the reason I wanted the position was that I had convinced myself it was more of a real estate-focused position. I have a long career working with my husband in more traditional residential real estate where I get the opportunity to help people achieve their economic empowerment goals via home ownership. It turned out the promotion was more compliance-focused, as opposed to empowering others. I did not have enthusiasm for that position.

As a long-term human resources leader, I have supported thousands of employees in various work streams and occupational areas. During my career, I have also supervised over a hundred employees either directly or via subordinate supervisors. This experience has provided me with the opportunity to interact with a variety of individuals around the world of work in blue-collar, white-collar, and entrepreneurial career paths. I have observed that work done well brings a sense of personal accomplishment, as we put our God-given talents and abilities to use.

Cinderella is a woman who is designed for greatness but doesn't know it. Imagine if we all knew who we were in relation to our vocation, or if we had all the information related to the blueprint for our life's work?

According to Angus Young, director at Prime Reason, a talent and management firm, "If a business maps individual performance, skills, and output within the organization, it will find that most of its employees do not meet the requirements for their roles. All people have unlimited potential. In other words, everyone has the right foot—it's the employer's responsibility to ensure we fit them into the right shoe."

I started my career as a 14-year-old file clerk working for an insurance firm in New York City's Wall Street District. Because I'm an optimist, I tend to repress traumatic experiences in my life but I remember two things as clear as day: the address was 55 Water Street, and I was thrilled to have my first job and earn my own money. I also vaguely remember a female manager at the firm requesting a specific file from me. I ran as quickly as I could to get the file, but I made a mistake and brought back the wrong one. She yelled at me and made me feel inadequate and embarrassed. To this day, that incident reminds me to treat all people with dignity and respect, regardless of their actions or poor performance.

A theme in the Cinderella story is the opposing concepts of work: rags (living as a maid) and riches (living as a princess) and a happily-ever-after ending. I compare that to the Employee vs. Entrepreneur dichotomy. In my opinion, entrepreneurship is often romanticized. Cinderella is, of course, a classic fairy story, a 'rags to riches' tale about a nice girl who suffers various hardships only to marry the Prince of the kingdom. The employee-to-entrepreneur journey is often seen as a linear process. Whether you are an entrepreneur or an employee, realize that you are responsible for caring for yourself and your family.

At the end of the day, I choose to bet on me. Why am I so confident? Fully leveraging career assessments has been critical. According to Wikipedia, "Career assessments are tools designed to help individuals understand how a variety of personal attributes (i.e., data values, preferences, motivations, aptitudes, and skills), impact their potential success and satisfaction with different career options and work environments."

I have been both a student and a practitioner of career assessments. I am an Administrator of the DiSC behavioral instruments system; DISC is the acronym for Dominance, Influence, Steadiness and Compliance. The test takers' answers are charted on a graph that breaks down these four behaviors. It looks at indicators like how you respond to challenges and how well you work with others. I am also certified to provide the Myers Briggs and Career Direct assessments.

The case for both entrepreneur and employee mindsets: my thesis is neither for, nor against, entrepreneurship versus employee. Why do I say that? I have lived in both worlds. As I transition from a full-time employee/part-time entrepreneur to a full-time business owner, I truly believe my design has always been entrepreneurial. Using this design in the workplace added value to my employment.

The most crucial step is to assess yourself and move towards work artistry—aligning your traits with the business analysis tool of assessing your strengths and weaknesses and connecting them with a framework for your best self. As I look at my personality and link it to my skills of being a human resource leader and a real estate practitioner, and my interests in economic development and people, I realize I am uniquely qualified to bring value. When assessing my entrepreneurship value proposition, I believe the skills that I have picked up as a 35-year employee are truly invaluable. I see a lot of it is the DNA coming from both worlds and I completely respect both entrepreneurs and employees.

My maternal grandmother and mother immigrated to this country from Costa Rica, for a better life, and were lifelong employees. My grandmother cleaned houses and retired as a maid from the famed Waldorf Astoria Hotel in New York City. My mother studied hard, became a clerk, graduated from community college, and retired as a registered nurse supervisor. My father was designed to be an entrepreneur. He migrated from South Carolina to New York, where he met my mother and worked as a parking lot attendant, but later owned parking garages and other businesses with my uncles. My grandmother and my parents made a decision and moved to the next level.

During my career in human resources, I have had several experiences where I felt like Cinderella. Because Human Resources itself is viewed as a support function, as opposed to the primary mission of the organization, the function itself can be seen as expendable, even if you are in an executive role. Human Resources positions are often viewed as an expense rather than an investment.

As Oprah Winfrey once said "You can have it all. Just not all at once." I believe that. Although I have been an employee for most of my working life, at the time of writing this chapter, I will be transitioning to my encore career as a Human Resources/Career Planning and Real Estate Practitioner via my firm, GPS Career and Business Strategies. In addition, I will offer real estate investing services via GPS Real Estate Solutions.

Neither entrepreneurship nor employment is positive or negative. It just is. Whether entrepreneur or employee, there are recommended steps to follow to take control of your vocation. To begin with, you need to clearly understand yourself.

- *First*, determine your design by assessing your personality, interests, skills, and values.

- *Second*, analyze the results of your assessment.

- *Third*, reflect on these results and discuss them with individuals whose opinions you value and trust. As in the world of Cinderella, perhaps it involves your fairy godmother (aka your career planning coach or guide).

- *Fourth*, decide if your personality, interests, values, and skills closely align with being an employee, an entrepreneur, or both?

- *Fifth*, research available opportunities in your design.

- Develop an action plan to determine your path so you can prepare.

- Determine your gaps. What resources will you need? What are your milestones for success? What are your target dates for completion for each milestone? Develop a training/resource plan for each gap you have identified.

- Last but not least, implement an action plan.

I must be an excellent steward of my time and talents but first, I must know what they are. As an employee, you are effectively selling your skills. As an entrepreneur, you are selling a set of skills that, no matter what, you must monetize. As an entrepreneur, a percentage of your business is being capitalized.

An additional lesson from the Cinderella story is to possess the work ethic of Cinderella. She gets on with the work, at times overwhelmed, but she recognizes the value of getting the job done—after all, so many people are relying on her. While reviewing my gaps is important, I must implement a training plan to mitigate my risks.

Identifying others committed to career planning goals, and joining accountability groups with a similar mission, may assist us in accomplishing our goals.

Cinderella provides an excellent framework for maintaining a vision of who you desire to be and, despite your circumstances, being committed to the work it may take to achieve your goals. We must realize it takes work to complete these goals. If you don't take the necessary, concrete action steps to assess who you are currently, and where you desire to be as related to your vocation, the chances of your achieving those career dreams will be bleak.

Please remember, the time is now. In the words of Mother Teresa, *"Yesterday is gone. Tomorrow has not yet come. We have only today. Let us begin."*

*"Your passion is your life's purpose
seeking outward expression."*

~ Bob Snyder

The words, "don't tell anyone," silenced **Jackie Bailey** at the age of eight. Fifteen years later, she saved another child by speaking up. Known as The International Conversation Coach, Jackie inspires her clients to break their silence and become victorious over trauma.

Today she is the founder and executive director of The Speak Feed Lead Project which has empowered hundreds of children, teens, and adults with confident, courageous voices shared on global stages, competitions, podcasts, and books.

Jackie is a 2015 semi-finalist in the World Championship of Public Speaking and a TEDx speaker.

**Website: jackiebailey360.com**

# Chapter 6

# Happily *Even* After . . .

## Jackie Bailey

*"Words are the most powerful drug used by mankind."*
~ Rudyard Kipling

*nce upon a time . . .*
Most fairy tales begin with these all-too-familiar words. For many people trauma happens more than once, leaving the victim unable to escape, trapped in a life they'd never choose.

### *. . . happily, ever after*

Often used as the closing phrase of a fairytale story plot, these three little words have set generations up for grave disappointment. We may live every day thinking happiness is one relationship or one rescue away. Thanks a lot, Snow White, Cinderella, and Princess Aurora.

### *Where is that white horse?*

Life is not a fairytale, and we've learned by now that if we ever dreamed of that happily-ever-after we aren't going to get it. Too many events derail the notion of *forever* happiness. However, the lesson I've learned and will share in this chapter, is that there is a way to live happily, even after devastating challenges. Grab your saddle, because *you* are the hero on the white horse.

### Three little words

From about the age of eight, I would be awakened in the middle of the night hearing his ankles crack outside my bedroom door. I'd plead, *Please, God, don't let it happen again.* I'd tuck my blankets tight around me so it would not be easy for the *beast* of my *scarytale*—my older brother—to complete his evil deed. When it was over, he would always warn:

### Don't tell anyone

I didn't. Those three little words made me cautious to initiate conversations, afraid I might *tell* something I shouldn't. I was silenced and swindled out of childhood. This more-than-once-upon-a-time trauma continued throughout my adolescence. Then, the clock struck midnight. The beast and his beauty (my brother and his wife) had a baby girl.

I was married by then with two young children. It may have appeared I was living a fairytale life, but I was merely managing unhappiness—as if the real me had been locked in some ogre's dungeon. I alone knew the secret threat lying in wait for that precious newborn child. If the glass slipper of silence was to be broken, I would have to break it. Besides metaphorically having a bloody foot, I had a lot at risk.

1. Revealing my secret would bring shame to my marriage and risk the stability of my so-called family life. Once my husband knew the curse I lived under, he might not want to be married to me.

2. Breaking the silence would bring shame to my brother and to my entire family. What if no one believed me and they tried to take my kids away?

3. If I stayed silent forever, by taking my own life, I'd cast a spell upon my children and they'd live in the shame of their mother's final decision, never knowing why.

4. Saying nothing and living life as I always had would be like a sword of shame being run through my heart. I could never be happy.

Taking a bite of that poisoned apple, I uttered three little words to my husband:

### I've a secret

My husband believed me. He supported my desire to heal. Next, I broke my silence to those whom I felt would advocate for me. I was believed by most; discounted by a few. At least my disclosure forced awareness about the beastly acts of my abuser and saved the life of the damsel in distress (my niece). I recognized increasingly the power of my voice when sharing my secret. I was being heard for the first time. (Cinderella taught us how a pair of shoes, or even one glass slipper, can change a girl's life.)

### You killed me

I read these words to my sibling abuser while confronting him face-to-face. It was a letter I had written directly to him. It read in part:

*You killed me. You murdered my soul while taking from me, without permission, what was most precious. You used me for pleasure and left me poisoned, slowly dying, unable to dream, and feeling forever unsafe.*

*Now you have a daughter. Will you take from her what you took from me? If I hear you have, I will take her from YOU any way I can."*

I told my beastly brother about the humiliation, the fear, and the awful shame I still lived with. A year or two before then, I could not have imagined being able to articulate my agony. My brother promised me he would never hurt his daughter. I learned he had confessed his sins to three different authority figures, outside of our parents, when I was 14 years old.

Since my brother's sins had been committed in the middle of the night when I was "asleep," and often included voyeuristic behavior of which I was unaware, he told these religious authorities that I didn't know. Each minister he spoke to—in higher and higher degrees of authority, over a period of months—repeated the same conclusion: *"If Jackie doesn't know, there is no harm done. You are forgiven."*

There had been no white horse for me. No breaking of a curse for my brother. The silence had been amplified for both of us. Still, a small seed of compassion for my brother was planted in the garbage heap of our lives. I was inching closer to the holy grail of healing. Like King Arthur, I was about to discover my mission.

### I forgive you . . .

My therapist cautioned me early on, "Jackie . . . *if you are not working toward forgiveness, you will never heal from the trauma you've suffered."*

I chuckled at the suggestion of forgiving then. It seemed as impossible as picking up a garbage truck and throwing it across the road. Years passed before I realized I, indeed, had reached this pinnacle of healing. The garbage truck had shrunk in size, and the seed of compassion planted years before was now reaping a harvest of forgiveness. The curse on the enchanted castle had been lifted.

The beast still needed saving, however. For years, my brother had been in and out of marriages, jobs, and . . . jail. He needed a different life and I was the only one who could give him that. Without my forgiveness, he would always be the beast.

I traveled more than 1,000 miles to say three little words. By stating *I forgive you* the sufferer had become the savior; the criminal had become the casualty. Healing was completed for me; healing had commenced for him. Forgiveness freed both the abused and the abuser. The beast finally had permission to heal, and he did.

- ***Don't tell anyone***—Hurtful words which altered the life of an innocent child.

- ***I've a secret***—Powerful words which converted pain into potential.

- ***You killed me***—Courageous words, describing sins and their awful effects.

- ***I forgive you***—Healing words which restored love, reversed wrong, and returned power to two unlikely characters.

Three little words spoken at contrasting times through the phases of my life's tale. To some, the words are insignificant but they are a symbolic depiction of the power of voice. Words took away my power; then words became my superpower. It is my life's purpose to help children, teens, and trauma survivors don their superhero capes and recognize the influence their voices have on everyone who hears them.

### *Speak Feed Lead*

These three little words represent the mission of *The Speak Feed Lead Project*, which I founded, and which prepares adults and children to share their heartfelt messages with the world in conversations at home, through podcasting, and keynoting on stages. Our clients *Speak* with power, *Feed* others in word and deed, and *Lead* with positive influence.

In 2020, *The National Children's Alliance* reported more than 600,000 abuse cases involving children in the United States. Furthermore, an estimated 1,750 of those children died from abuse—silenced forever . . . in most cases, by family members. If we consider the unreported cases, the number of children affected climbs significantly. But, even based on what we do know, that leaves more than half a million kids every year who likely live in silence like I did.

As a survivor of childhood sexual, physical, and emotional abuse, I know trauma will chronically gnaw away at your self-esteem, self-love, and self-fulfillment year after year; relationship after relationship; and experience after experience. I will not allow children to be silenced, if I can help it. I will empower them to speak up. I delight in helping adults understand that their voice and powerful message will be their healing balm. Being a metaphorical fire-breathing keynote speaker will slay the dragon of their inner, frightened child.

### *Find Your Power*

Even from an early age, I knew the abuse was wrong. Despite being powerless to stop it I did have power over my reaction to it. I remember thinking to myself, *If I live through this, I will be strong.* Now I know I was already strong. I was a good kid, even though my mother didn't think so and accused me of awful things. Her mistrust of me was unwarranted.

I regret not helping a friend who was bullied and beaten in front of me one day when I was eleven years old. Fear of being targeted myself kept me from speaking up for my friend and standing up for her. I vowed to never back down from injustice again. We may not always be able to stand up for ourselves as abuse victims, but we do have the power to stand up for others. We can impact the lives of others through our words, prayers, and actions. We are all more powerful than we know.

### *Break Your Silence*

As I began therapy (which I highly recommend), I learned the power of writing. I'd always been a journal keeper, and my therapist taught me writing as a healing tool. Since remaining silent about trauma will deepen the effects, it's important to break the silence when you can—even if it's through writing. Write about your feelings. Describe what's happened to you. Write a letter to your nemesis, tell him or her how they've hurt you, and express the ways you are stronger than they are. Make a list of who you would break the silence to if you were brave enough and ready for it.

After writing, keep it, tear it up, or burn it. Do whatever feels most empowering to you. You may even send it to someone. If you're not yet ready to break the silence verbally, there is strength in writing. And, when you are ready to speak out, I suggest choosing a person to tell who will most likely believe and support you. Break your silence in the most empowering way for YOU.

## Confront the Enemy

This step is optional and should be taken only if it's safe to face the person who has been the cause of your trauma. DO NOT do this alone. Have a support person with you when the confrontation happens. Your support person should not have a dog in the fight, such as a spouse. If a crime has been committed, I suggest you have law enforcement at your side. Your priority is to maintain safety for yourself and your family.

On the day I confronted my brother, I arranged for Shelly (a neighbor) to sit next to me while I read my letter to him. Shelly did not have to say or do anything, just be there for moral support. I found strength in breaking through the fear of reading my written letter to my brother. I didn't have to make eye contact, but I was able to say exactly what I wanted to for the very first time. It was emotionally painful and extremely purging! Like taking out the garbage.

## Live to Forgive

You do not have to forgive tomorrow, next year, or even before you die. The most meaningful and powerful aspect of your healing journey will be to work toward forgiving. That's all. Consider the possibility. Forgiveness doesn't mean you condone what was done, and it doesn't wipe the slate clean regarding a relationship with your abuser. It does mean the other person no longer rents space in your head, your heart, or your future. You can let it go.

After I spent time in therapy alone, I joined a group of 15 other women survivors. Carol was a special member of the group. During hypnosis, she remembered being raped at the age of three and suffocated to death with a pillow. Carol recalled sitting with a person she knew as *Heavenly Father* who told her she had died but would be going back. *Heavenly Father* explained to Carol that He was going to provide others who would help her survive and cope with her pain.

When Carol reunited with her body, she had 32 personalities, ranging from infants to dangerous thugs. They were gifts, and took on particular roles which Carol was not able to handle. For 35 years, Carol was unaware of her many helpers, since she'd black out when one of them showed up. Those of us in the group had witnessed them. During our therapy sessions, I played with the children who lived inside Carol and experienced fearful moments with the male bouncers who aggressively guarded Carol whenever memories threatened her.

I was honored to be with Carol when she integrated her personalities during hypnosis. The process Carol walked through is a lesson for all of us. One by one, in her mind's eye, Carol would visualize and address each personality face-to-face and describe to each one how they had played a part in her healing journey. Lastly, Carol would hug them and thank each one for their support. *"I don't need you anymore,"* she would say. *"I'm strong enough to do this on my own."*

Carol bid farewell to each character as they integrated back into her core personality. Goodbye Elizabeth, Roger, Baby Jane, and Tootie. I don't fully understand the mental science behind what I witnessed Carol accomplish throughout several sessions of therapy, but I do know she had to reach a level of healing before she was ready for such an important step.

We must all do what Carol did (multiple personalities or not). Forgiveness happens when we can look at each emotion we've endured through our abuse and the process of healing, and find the gifts. There is so much that can be dusted up during years of therapy. Just like Carol, we can reach the point when we feel gratitude for the meaningful ways we've been shaped by our trauma. Then, we can figurately give each emotion, trait, and attitude a hug and send it on its way. "Bye-bye anger, shame, pain, humiliation, injury, and hatred. I don't need you anymore. I can take it from here."

## *Postscript*

You may be wondering, *What about your niece, Jackie?* Thanks for asking. Twenty years post-forgiveness, in a moment of weakness, my brother made a horrible mistake. My niece was 30 years old when her dad was arrested for a crime against a child she knew. Feeling confused and conflicted, she gave me a call.

*"Aunt Jackie, how could my dad do something like that?"*

Her question indicated my brother had kept his promise to me to never hurt her! It was a tender mercy for me since we don't often know if our actions have a positive outcome for others. I shared with my niece what I knew about her dad, and how it related to me. I helped her understand why she was never allowed to be alone with him, and why he couldn't spend time with her as other fathers would do. Despite my brother's arrest and the devastating sadness I felt for another victim, I was elated by three little words my niece said to me:

### You Saved Me

I had shown up years before on a white horse. I had broken the generational curse of abuse, poor communication, and silencing. Using my voice had slayed a dragon. My words had mattered for one child. Your words matter for the child in you. Your powerful, healing, hero's journey should be shared.

Three little words in my life have come to represent the power of communication to either crush or lift the spirit. My trauma happened more than *once upon a time*, and I stopped looking for the *happily, ever after.*

Now I know no matter what tragedy, trauma, or challenge we face, there is the possibility of living *happily, EVEN after.*

Break your silence. The beginning . . .

**Mila Johansen** is a public speaker, writing and publishing coach, teacher, and writer. She is the best-selling author of nine books, including, *From Cowgirl to Congress: Journey of a Suffragist on the Front Lines*. A first-person account from Jessie Haver Butler, Mila's grandmother who was the first woman lobbyist in D.C. and taught public speaking to 1,000s of women including Eleanor Roosevelt. In her early 90s, Jessie shared the podium several times with Gloria Steinem and Marlo Thomas and took Mila along.

Mila also has several more books in progress and loves to write and produce short screenplays. She has developed "The Short Book" concept giving people all over the world permission to write and publish their "short book" first.

Now she is helping many people write and publish their books, making the process easy and accessible. She loves to work in any genre, including anthologies and cookbooks, making people's dreams of becoming published authors come true.

Email: johansenmila@gmail.com
Website: milajohansen.com

## Chapter 7

# Yikes! Get Me
# to College—*Quick!*

### Mila Johansen

*"Going to school—picking an apple.*
*Getting an education—eating it."*
~ E.L. Konigsburg

From my diary, after high school graduation: *Okay, done with high school. Headed to college. Wait a minute— got a job offer in factory across the street from my house. Tired of school anyway—gonna take it with Ronnie, employed there too. My best friend Ronnie's mother works there and got us the jobs. It's called Hagen and Renaker and they produce little porcelain animals—really cute minuscule beasts with apparent personalities. Wow—they sell all over the world. I am going to be an independent woman of means and I only have to open my front door and walk across the street.* The perfect after-high-school-graduation job—or so I thought.

So we sat there, day after day, with little knives carving off tiny lines left over from the molds that the clay slip had been poured into. First, they gave us the supposedly easy ones—bunnies. Little, cute, wet bunnies—grey—no bigger than the end of my pinky finger. One problem, they all had pointy ears—ears that stuck straight up. On my first tray of twenty, I broke off most of the ears. By my second tray, I had only mutilated half of the unsuspecting, innocent victims. Eventually, after many exasperating looks, followed by impatient huffs from the floor managers who supplied the endless parade of animal kingdom replicas—I got better. Not much better. Ronnie improved at a rapid rate—DNA from her mother, I suppose—as I crept along, slow as a tortoise traveling to market.

Finally, after several months of this grueling, painful means of employment, they brought me a tray of the . . . ta-da . . . deer. I had graduated to the next level in the fake animal kingdom. Not the bucks yet, with their delicate tree of antlers—most excellent, waiting to be broken, antlers— but they decided to trust me with the does. The does proved hard enough—with four long, spindly legs begging my fingers to snap each one as my work knife carved up and down their thin, extended appendages. Oh crap—I broke every leg on the entire tray! *Surely they will fire me and release me from this eternal hell.*

Did I mention that I received a grand total of minimum wage? $1.60. And to entice me further, everyone there discussed, ad nauseam, how much I would make—in excruciating increments—as time went by. Oh my goodness! I could work my way up to $3.50 an hour if I was diligent and stuck to it for several years. Whoops, I mean *centuries.* My future was laid out before me—all neatly mapped out as if I were attending medical school. I could sit there in that waiting chair for decades, employed by a miniature clay zookeeper industry. All this glory promised to me as if it were the golden rectangle at the end of the yellow brick road. The Holy Grail of womanhood. The pot of gold at the end of the grownup rainbow. Go girl—you can sit here for the rest of your life and rot like the rest of us.

Now if that wasn't impetus to go—no, I mean RUN! to college—nothing was.

## First Stop Junior College

I thought I might be going to a regular four-year college. That is often what's on the minds of high school seniors. Surprise! I'm going to confess to you what might have become an awkward moment for most, but which I was impervious to. Because I grew up in gangland, on the outskirts of Los Angeles, surrounded and enticed by constant opportunities to ditch school for alternate, sometimes dangerous, activities, I graduated high school with a C– grade point average. Shocked? Don't be. It turned out that I was one of the only kids in my neighborhood and friend bank to go to college— and later graduate from a four-year college. Believe it or not, back then to attend a four-year college, you only needed a C plus average. So I went to junior college first to bring up my grade point average.

Turns out college is an entirely different planet from the stilted halls of high school purgatory. I learned one thing in high school. Typing. I am a kinesthetic learner and now I can type 70 words a minute—not accurately—but it is a very good skill for a writer to have.

Junior college turned out to be the perfect maturing ground for me. Looking back, I can honestly say that the teachers at Mount San Antonio Junior College in Pomona,

California were the top of the line. Every one of them taught with energy and passion and instilled in me a lifelong excitement for learning.

Later, when I arrived at Chico State in Northern California, half the teachers were pumped up to teach and the others were half-dead, with eyes glazed over, waiting for their tenure to turn into retirement. So, hey everyone, tell every young person you know to savor the time they spend in junior college.

My poetry teacher started the class by reading a poem she had written about a very intimate moment with herself in her youth. That surprising reading set the pace for the class and we all became brave in our own writings and what we shared. I became a poet.

My favorite teacher was in philosophy. One of the oddest, most fascinating people I have ever met. He told us how he slept in a water tank, shaped like a coffin, floating through the night into dreamland. I became a philosopher. I still wonder—if there is no one in the forest to hear it, does the falling tree make a noise?

Then, because of my grandmother, a famous public speaker who taught Eleanor Roosevelt public speaking, I was selected to join the traveling Speech Team. I also joined the Debate Team, and I became very good at it. I became a speaker.

Being a starving student, the profound thought came to me . . . *why aren't all the trees on campus fruit trees?* I don't think I had many deep thoughts back then. My generation, as a whole, grew up very naïve. We had no internet or smart T.V. dramas to educate us socially. We were left to manage as best we could, raising one another in our cars, in the parks, and up in the hills. Meanwhile, our parents carried on without us in Parents Without Partners, entertaining new spouses, or attending adult-only parties.

I remember another profound thought that occurred to me. I have no idea what prompted it, and even though it is now a totally viable solution to the overpopulation of the planet, I'm still surprised that my 19-year-old self came up with it. I thought of graveyards, golf courses, and schoolyards as a way to preserve plots of land to grow food inside cities and townships of the future. And now landscapers everywhere are planting food-growing plants outside of office buildings instead of ornamental shrubs.

During junior college, I held down two jobs. One of them was working in the kitchen at a prominent convalescent home. On my first day, the friendly, well-endowed head cook handed me a flyswatter and instructed me to kill as many flies as possible. Being a tender heart, and never having murdered anything on purpose, I went around pretending to swat the irritating beasties. Smack! Pop! I'm still that way, rescuing worms from the sidewalks in the rain, and removing insects from the house with cups and paper towels. But mosquitoes beware. Anyone who wants to suck my blood will be executed!

Having been the Cinderella in our family since the age of ten, and often performing four hours of housework a day, the head cook appreciated my dedication to each task. She quickly promoted me to a more interesting job, formerly held by a member of the male persuasion—Head Dishwasher—the first female to ever hold that coveted position. The position gave me more freedom and I even got to drive the delivery cart with trays of meals for other sections of the massive senior complex. I got to escape the confines of the sweltering kitchen for long periods of time. I loved manning the massive dishwashing equipment and felt accomplished, and in charge, in my stainless-steel domain.

## Shoved in the Right Direction

Late in my second year of Junior College, my friend, Janine, burst into the dining room where I was clearing the dishes from several tables. "I just heard of an amazing college up North—Chico State—and we're going to go."

I stared at her, stunned; Janine had never attended college or even talked about college as an option. But her enthusiasm infused me, and I filled out the application she waved in front of my face and sent it in the next day. She never went to college, but I—with my stick-to-itiveness and total follow-through, armed with my new C+ average—was accepted.

I was on my way to Chico State in northern California—so I thought. One problem, my mother refused to help me out monetarily and I couldn't go. Believe it or not, the cost to attend state colleges back then was only $400 a year, plus room and board.

When I told my grandmother that Rosemary refused to help me, she flipped! She told my mother off like no one in the world could do. She reminded Rosemary that she had paid huge amounts for her to attend the most prestigious colleges when she was a young adult. She told Rosemary that she would never speak to her again if she didn't give her own daughter the same chance at higher education that was provided for her.

The following January, yes, January, I found myself packed onto a bus, with my Motobecane ten-speed bicycle strapped onto the rear end, and on the way to my future. Remember, I started junior college mid-semester, after quitting my prestigious factory job, and so graduated with my A.A. right before the Christmas holiday that year.

I don't think it was in my mother's DNA or vocabulary to drive me to my new school like other parents might have felt compelled to do. I now think that she might have been relieved to get rid of me.

I felt a mixture of emotions: excitement, fear, loneliness, and trepidation. I arrived at the Chico bus station and called a taxi. The driver, an elderly, friendly fellow, said, "Welcome to the Town of Trees." Indeed, massive trunks rose up before me in every direction with splays of luscious, green foliage blocking out the sky. I never heard that term again.

He dropped me off at my pre-arranged new home—an off-campus dorm. The dean quickly installed me in a room with three other girls. They didn't seem thrilled to see me and frankly, never warmed up to the idea of me sharing their four-bedroom space. Aloof and preppy in their ways, they provided no welcoming words or invitations. I soon realized the folly of joining a school year already set in motion.

At first, I floundered, not sure where, or if, I fit in. I rode my bike—my only mode of transportation—through the flat streets, exploring my new hometown. I didn't feel at home. I couldn't shake off the extreme loneliness that permeated my very soul. I remember that I started wishing a car would hit me and put me out of my misery. I had never had those thoughts before, or ever again, and I knew it was totally unacceptable. I wrote thirty letters, to everyone I knew, in those first few weeks. Some wrote back.

That sense of desperation only lasted two weeks. For one thing, the food was abundant and delicious. Three meals a day and I didn't have to prepare any of it. Cinderella, now relieved of her duties, had a kitchen full of workers taking care of her. She didn't have to clean anything. A sense of freedom set in and hope teased her out of her depression.

Then I made a friend. I went into the large living room and sat on the couch to watch T.V. "Mash" was on. The girl next to me struck up a conversation and we became friends for life. We later shared a room in a house together and now we still live in the same town with a vibrant friendship. She saved me. She got me and liked me the very first minute we met. She still gets me. I have to admit, I am a bit of an odd egg and people either get me or they don't.

A funny story is that we scored a huge room in the back of a house, for the low cost of $70 a month—$35 each, where we danced, ate Cream of Wheat for dinner, and invited friends over. We were both so naïve that we didn't realize that the young men who rented us the room were the biggest drug dealers in Chico. We never even wondered why so many "friends," (a constant stream of people) went in and out of the house and the back cottage. It just wasn't on our radar . . . until it was. We soon realized that a drug bust might get us incarcerated as well. We moved out at the end of that year.

## Singled Out

Then I met *him*. We had each joined the same intramural coed baseball team that a mutual friend had put together. I showed up for the very first game of the season and no one came but one person, Rich. We had never met before that day and started talking. Instantly, within five minutes, I wanted to be part of his life. For some reason I felt a certain calm, and that his bedroom and house would be organized and welcoming—not in a sexual way. I know that sounds corny, but I wanted to be part of it.

We finally had to officially forfeit the game since only two of us showed up. We shrugged and began walking in different directions—me home, and he headed towards the campus buildings. I suddenly turned around, caught up to him, and said, "Where are you going?" He said he wanted to work on his painting in the art department. I went along to see his work. I told him I had a weekly dancing date that night with my girlfriend and asked if he wanted to meet me there. He did, and we started dating.

He courted me by dropping boxes of oranges off on my doorstep, a relief to my roommate and me because we were mostly subsisting on Cream of Wheat and popcorn. Later, I married him. He's an organic farmer, so I never went hungry again. We've been married for forty-three years now—one of the main abundances of my life. By the way, the rest of the team showed up to every other game after that fateful day.

When I met my husband, Rich, he put me to work on his family's ranch. Luckily for him, he got "Cinderella" because I had done that four hours a day of work at my house growing up. When I saw all the fruit, and the number twos (substandard for selling), I said, "Rich, there's so much extra fruit, we've got to give it away."

He said, "No, no, no, Mila. We don't give anything away." Rich is the most generous person I know, but his family came out of the Depression era and lived in that consciousness, even though they earned very good money, and owned several businesses.

I insisted, "Oh yeah, we're going give it away." In the long run, I won out and now we give 10,000 to 20,000 pounds a year to local food banks.

Another abundance that occurred during that period was that, while attending college on a very meager budget, I couldn't afford red meat. I ate chicken, which was half the price. After one school year of not eating red meat, as soon as I got home that summer, I ordered a roast beef sandwich. My stomach was not used to digesting the dense substance and I doubled over for two hours in extreme pain. So, I never ate red meat again. As you can see, it wasn't for religious reasons or anything. I am so happy that I have only eaten fish, chicken, and plant proteins for the past forty-seven years.

But here's the odd thing, I married into the last remaining slaughterhouse in northern California. Yikes! Rich's family owns the citrus ranch, and in another part of town, a slaughterhouse. The first day he brought me to meet his family, we stopped at the slaughterhouse first. They were butchering six goats, hanging from hooks with maroon droplets of blood splattering on the cement floor. I stood there in shock and utter disgust. I had never given any thought to where meat came from, or how the animals were killed, or any of it. Then and there, I vowed to never eat red meat again and I haven't—not even one bite. Rich had nothing to do with the slaughterhouse. His side of the family ran the organic citrus ranch, and the other side ran the slaughterhouse and butcher shop.

Before I close this chapter about my predestined college days, (thank you Janine), I must tell you about our very avant-garde honeymoon. We were married barefoot in a park in Monterey California, after dipping into the ocean. For our honeymoon, we hiked through Haleakala, the volcano on Maui—29 miles downhill, bracing ourselves with our heavy backpacks on. We spent the first night in the Sierra Club cabin, halfway through the volcano, and then camped on the beach in Hana, running naked through the jungles, and jumping the cliffs of the Seven Sacred Pools.

And that is the true story of one Cinderella, propelled into college where she met the love of her life—her destiny set in motion at an intramural baseball game.

**Irma Goosen** is a TEDx speaker, author, and Toastmasters leader. She brings a wealth of experience from her immigration journey: moving from South Africa to the U.S., and finally, to Canada.

She shares her insights in her guide, "Surviving Culture Shock," and extends her literary talent to Young Adult fiction.

A proponent of impactful communication and personal growth, Irma blends her tech savvy and community building passion, highlighted in her dynamic stage presence and the innovative C.O.N.N.E.C.T. concept she pioneered.

**Contact: linktr.ee/irmagoosen**

## Chapter 8

# 1 Dream, 2 Suitcases, 3 Countries:
### *The leap of faith to finding a new home*
#### Irma Goosen

*"When we enlighten today's society about
legal immigration, we light the path
for tomorrow's harmony."*

~ Irma Goosen

Have you ever caught yourself musing about the sheer audacity it would take to abandon the familiar comfort of your home? To vacate every nook and cranny of your life, and set out with nothing but the weight of dreams and a couple of suitcases? To find a life where you could sleep without the bulge of a weapon underneath your pillow?

I was born and raised in the expansive landscapes of South Africa, a country where the sun paints the sky with its generous golden hues almost every day. The vibrant culture is as vast and diverse as the land itself, echoing the rhythms of its many tribes and the harmonies of its multi-faceted histories. Wildlife, a testament to nature's grandeur, roams freely in vast reserves, reminding us of the wild heart that beats within the continent. Yet, amidst this beauty and richness, there exists a paradox. In some corners, the value of life is diminished, overshadowed by struggles and conflicts that contrast starkly with the country's inherent opulence and beauty.

It is this juxtaposition of beauty and hardship, of dreams and realities, that often fuels the desire to seek new horizons. Many, like me, look beyond our borders, compelled by various reasons, hoping for change, growth, or escape. And this isn't a sentiment unique to South Africans.

According to the United Nations, I am not alone in this journey. Every year, hundreds of millions traverse borders, bidding goodbye to their native lands and embracing new horizons. They leave for opportunities, for education, for the promise of a brighter tomorrow. My personal narrative is intertwined with such global stories. Born in the heart of South Africa, my path took me first to the bustling cities of the United States and later, the tranquil snow-covered landscapes of Canada.

However, I am more than a mere statistic on a chart. My narrative is a tapestry woven with threads of discovery, hope, trepidation, and resilience. It tells of a daunting voyage: the rebuilding of a home and a life from the very foundation.

Leaving South Africa, the land of my birth and the keeper of my earliest memories, was akin to tearing a page from a cherished book. The vibrancy of its culture, the warmth of the sun, and the familiarity of its voices had been my cocoon. As my plane soared away, I felt an amalgamation of excitement, trepidation, and melancholy. I was eager for the new experiences the United States promised, yet a part of me mourned what I was leaving behind.

My initial days in the US were a whirlwind of adjustments. The fast-paced life, the melting pot of cultures, and the vastness of its cities were both enthralling and overwhelming. The challenges were many: from understanding the nuances of American slang to navigating the intricacies of their bureaucratic systems. But with every stumble, there were also moments of joy and realization. I cherished the friendships I forged, the myriad opportunities the country offered, and the broadening of my world perspective.

Yet, as time wore on, a new calling emerged. Canada, with its promise of serene landscapes, diverse populace, and a different set of opportunities, beckoned. Transitioning from the US to Canada carried its own set of emotional weights. I was now leaving behind a country I had grown to love and understand, to once again dive into the unknown. The challenges in Canada were different from those in the US. The colder climes, the friendly yet reserved nature of its people, and the quieter pace of life were new terrains to navigate.

There were moments of stark realization: understanding that home isn't just a physical place, but a feeling you carry within; recognizing that every move, every change, molds you in imperceptible ways; and that, in the journey of life, adaptability is your strongest ally.

Through these transitions, from South Africa to the US, and then to Canada, I've learned that while lands and cultures may differ, the essence of humanity remains consistent. Emotions, dreams, and the quest for a better life are universal threads that bind us all.

In the bustling, diverse landscape of the United States, I discovered a passion that would shape the next phase of my life: working with the youth. The young minds, eager and impressionable, resonated with my own journey of adaptation and discovery. Their stories, struggles, and aspirations were mirrors reflecting varying shades of my own experiences. It became evident to me that these youths, regardless of their backgrounds, faced challenges in understanding their identities and aspirations, and navigating the complexities of the society around them.

It was during this time that the seeds of the CONNECT framework were sown. I realized that beyond academic guidance, there was a dire need for a holistic approach to help these youngsters integrate better, communicate more effectively, and build networks that would support their ambitions. Thus, step by step, the **CONNECT** framework took shape, each letter representing a crucial element of success in a new land: **<u>C</u>ommunication**, **<u>O</u>pen-<u>M</u>indedness**, **<u>N</u>etworking**, **<u>N</u>urturing** relationships, **<u>E</u>xploring** opportunities, **<u>C</u>ollaborating**, and **<u>T</u>hriving** amidst adversity.

The framework wasn't just limited to the youth. As I delved deeper, I recognized its universal appeal and its significant relevance to the topic of legal immigration. The principles embedded in CONNECT became tools to help immigrants understand, navigate, and succeed in their new homes. Equipped with this, I began my mission to educate individuals about the intricacies of legal immigration, emphasizing the human stories and shared experiences that underscore the statistics.

Today, the CONNECT framework isn't just a method; it's a movement. It's a testament to the power of shared human experiences, the importance of understanding and adapting, and the immense potential that lies within each of us, waiting to be harnessed. This 7-step methodology is not just an acronym; it's a beacon for every immigrant trying to find their way. It is a testament to the journey I've undertaken and the wisdom I've amassed.

Empowered by the success and potential of the CONNECT framework, I felt a compelling drive to share these insights and stories on a larger scale. It wasn't just about confined classrooms or community gatherings anymore; I envisioned arenas where the essence of my journey and the principles of the framework could resonate with thousands.

My foray into public speaking began with local stages. These initial events, while modest in scale, were monumental for me. They provided a space where I could refine my narrative, gauge audience reactions, and most importantly, affirm the universal relevance of the messages I carried. The applause and feedback post each speech were not just validations; they were catalysts urging me to aim higher.

However, as with all crafts, the art of public speaking demanded finesse, structure, and continual learning. This understanding led me to Toastmasters. In the supportive and constructively critical environment of Toastmasters, I honed my oratory skills, learning the nuances of captivating diverse audiences and molding my narrative to be more impactful. It became a training ground, shaping me for larger stages and grander audiences.

And then, the crowning moment arrived: an invitation to speak at TEDx in San Diego. The iconic red dot wasn't just a stage; it was a testament to my journey—from the vibrant landscapes of South Africa, through the bustling life in the US, to the reflective halls of Toastmasters, and the myriad stories and lessons along the way. Speaking at TEDx, I wasn't just sharing a framework or a personal tale; I was weaving a global narrative, highlighting the shared human experiences and the boundless possibilities that arise when we truly CONNECT.

My advocacy for immigrant success is deeply rooted in my experiences and fueled by the stories of countless others. One tale that resonates profoundly with me is that of a family who, driven by dreams of a better tomorrow, journeyed from the sun-soaked plains of South Africa to the bustling cities of the United States, and then, drawn by another calling, to Canada's icy embrace. This family's story is my family's story.

For us, each transition brought a fresh set of challenges and wonders. In the United States, the sprawling urban landscapes and the cacophony of diverse voices offered both excitement and moments of feeling adrift. The pace, the blend of cultures, and even the nuances of American English presented a world vastly different from our South African roots.

Yet, just as we began to find our footing in the U.S., the allure of Canada beckoned. Stepping onto Canadian soil, we were greeted by a different environment altogether. The cooler winds, vast expanses, and a more muted cultural tapestry initially felt like a stark contrast to both our South African heritage and our American experiences.

Every day was a mosaic of learning and unlearning. Adapting to new customs, understanding varying cultural underpinnings, and melding our rich South African background with the subtleties of North American life became our daily endeavor. It often seemed like we were trying to harmonize the vivacious rhythms of South Africa with the diverse melodies of the U.S. and the gentle refrains of Canada.

With time and tenacity, what once felt foreign gradually became familiar. Our story morphed from that of outsiders to one of integration, from observers to active participants in our communities. In this journey, our family's experiences became emblematic of the broader immigrant narrative—a testament to the shared struggles, joys, and resilient spirit of those who venture beyond their known horizons.

My tenure in the technical realm has further honed my skills, especially when it comes to articulating complex thoughts and concepts into speeches that resonate with a broad audience. Beyond professional pursuits, I've always believed in giving back to society. By volunteering at schools and architecting leadership programs for the youth, I aim to shape the leaders of tomorrow, ensuring they possess a global perspective and an empathetic heart.

One of my most cherished memories stems from a chilly winter afternoon at a local school in the heart of a small town called Okotoks, nestled in the Foothills of the Rocky Mountains. As part of a volunteering stint, I was scheduled to address a diverse group of young students, many of whom were recent immigrants. A bright-eyed girl, probably no older than 12, hesitantly approached me after my talk. With a quiver in her voice, she recounted her own migration journey and the challenges of adjusting to a new land. My story, she said, made her feel seen and understood. Months later, I learned that she spearheaded a multicultural club in her school, fostering understanding and collaboration among students from varied backgrounds. This was the ripple effect in action—a single story inspiring action and change.

My forays into creating leadership programs were similarly rooted in a desire to ignite such ripples. I recall a particularly impactful workshop where we simulated an 'immigration journey.' Participants navigated a series of challenges, akin to what immigrants face, fostering empathy and insight. One young man, visibly moved, later shared that the exercise gave him profound respect for his parents, who were immigrants themselves, and inspired him to document their journey for future generations.

Such instances reaffirmed the power of storytelling and mentorship. My motivation behind these initiatives has always been twofold: firstly, to provide the youth with the tools and mindset to navigate their challenges, and secondly, to create a more understanding and inclusive society. By instilling leadership qualities, promoting empathy, and spotlighting the immigrant narrative, I aim to cultivate a generation that not only respects diversity but champions it.

Our stories, intertwined with the landscapes we traverse and the people we meet, form the tapestry of our existence. From the sunbaked horizons of South Africa to the bustling life of the United States, and the tranquil embrace of Canada, my journey has been one of discovery, resilience, and connection. The paths I've walked, the challenges I've faced, and the lives I've touched along the way are testament to the power of human spirit and determination.

Whether it's through the CONNECT framework, advocacy for immigrant success, or empowering the next generation with leadership tools, my mission remains constant: to foster understanding, bridge divides, and illuminate the shared experiences that unite us all.

In a world replete with boundaries—both visible and invisible—it is our shared stories, our collective dreams, and our united efforts that will truly usher in a brighter, more inclusive tomorrow. As you turn this page, I invite you to reflect on your own journey, the stories you carry, and the bridges you can build. For in every story, in every endeavor, lies the potential to connect, inspire, and transform the world around us.

**Susan Nelson Gouveia** has been passionate about foraging the land for food and medicine ever since she was a child. She began cooking family meals when her mom cut her loose in the kitchen. She rarely ever watched TV and has an on-going lust for creativity.

"When I decided to be my authentic self, and go back to who I was at nine, my world changed and my tribe evolved. Today, I am living a passionate life with great friends, family, food, and creative projects."

Susan is currently a private chef and culinary teacher. She spends her days writing recipes, entertaining, homesteading, and learning new things at Garden Goddess Farm—her "university," as her son calls it.

**Website: gardengoddesses.org**

## Chapter 9

# Family & Food

### Susan Nelson Gouveia

*"Cooking with intention, love, and joy
is one of the best gifts you can give to yourself,
your family, and community."*
~ Susan Nelson Gouveia

My parents celebrate 60 years together this year. My love of food, especially as it brings family and friends together, is inspired by my parents' love of healthy food. Their stories about mealtime as they were growing up reveal why.

As the eldest daughter in a family of ten, my Mom remembers being frequently reminded of the expense of providing for eight hearty appetites. The goal was to "extend" every meal. She says, "Dad shopped with a keen eye for a deal and cooked to 'extend' each ingredient to a few dinners."

One-pot meals were standard, and meat was scarce, so spaghetti was flavored with watered-down tomato sauce and peppered with specks of hamburger. Stew was mostly potatoes, a couple of carrots, a stalk or two of celery, and the hunt was on for the bits of fatty meat. Other meals included: 'Pot of Beans'—just kidney beans, and his special 'Dutch pea soup'—a sickly, green color, thick enough to stand a spoon in. Cut up hot dogs in creamed corn was popular with the youngest kids. We'd alternate spaghetti and beans until finally, they were combined for yet another meal.

Breakfast never varied: mush—cornmeal or oatmeal. Lunch was just as predictable: egg or tuna salad sandwiches, spread so thin it would rip the bread.

Mom's happiest memory of food and family was running home when she smelled the weekly loaves of her mom's bread, ready to come out of the oven. A fresh, hot slice of bread was a favorite memory for all the kids and was the smell that kept the kids coming back to the house.

As the eldest son in a family of seven, my dad's life-long love of fishing—especially salmon fishing in the Monterey Bay—came from a revelation that fresh salmon in no way resembled his childhood Friday salmon loaf, which tasted like cat food and was required eating or he would surely go to hell! Equally horrible were Friday fish sticks, but those, at least, he could drown in ketchup.

As a reaction to these and other family meals, my parents raised my sister and me on freshly caught fish, and eggs from our own chickens. They grew fresh vegetables and fruit and, while we were on camping and fishing trips, they taught us a little about foraging and the pleasures of nature.

After my second divorce, I was feeling lost and disconnected from community. I felt a need to create my own tribe of like-minded people. I wasn't sure how to do this and was tired of book clubs. I started reflecting back to my childhood and realized I always loved getting my hands dirty. Some of my fondest childhood memories are of helping my grandmother in the garden, foraging the land with my Aunt Marie, and cooking delicious meals from whatever was harvested from our efforts. Decades later, I turned that love of gardening, and passion for cooking into a local institution—The Society of Garden Goddesses®, which was established in 2010. The group of both men and women has grown like wildflowers—almost doubling in size from the 750 members it had on November 4, 2016.

Suddenly, everyone wants to know how to grow their own food organically, and I'm so happy to have a forum to help them on that journey! We share tips, recipes, and lots of laughs! I wanted to take the seriousness and chore out of gardening and cooking and get people excited about experimenting with food grown in one's own garden. More than just a group of gardeners, this is a family. It is a "tribe" that gets together for fun events that include monthly garden tour potlucks, Happy Gardening Hour taste and learn events, holiday bazaars, volunteer projects, demos, classes, and much more.

A few years ago, I had two nearly fatal car accidents that clarified my life's mission. In one accident I rolled a Chevy Tahoe on the way to Lake Tahoe, and on the other I was rear ended by a drunk driver while waiting for the light to change—a mere five minutes from home. When that happened, I was so lucky to survive, and through the whole ordeal I felt that I was receiving a message from Spirit. I was told to commit to community, and that my role is to connect people, and bring back that sense of community through cooking and gardening together.

Over the years, I have added more than just gardening to my repertoire of services. I am a Private Chef and have studied with chefs in Spain, Mexico, India, Brazil, Italy, France, and Peru. I love to coach individuals who are wanting to learn a more sustainable way of living and eating.

In addition, I offer cooking classes and "Kitchen Coaching" at our farm culinary kitchen and online through video conferencing. Some students just need a little extra help in the kitchen or want to expand their culinary skills, and I feel honored that I am able to help them with that.

Never one to sit still, I continue working with the HoneyBee Foundation, mentoring teens in the culinary arts. Teenage years can be such an awkward time for kids. Teaching them about foraging the land, leadership, cooking, and community service is a great way to nurture a passion in them. We learn to honor each season and appreciate the bounty of each harvest.

I started this program when the kids were getting a bit bored and squirrely during the pandemic. One of my son's friends, Ryan, approached me and asked me to mentor him on an FFA project. He said he wanted to grow nopales cactus instead of raising animals to slaughter. What a genius! Other kids caught wind of this concept and they ended up collaborating on a successful spring plant sale! Additionally, some of the kids went on to become published authors and are pursuing plant-based diets and nutrition majors in college.

My son calls our farm "The University." There is so much to discover about native, edible California plants! I continue to experiment with plants and herbs and create new recipes daily. Additionally, I love solution-based activism, mentoring young adults, and inspiring people to create their tribe and build community.

We recently published our first book, *Recipes from the Garden Goddesses: For Cuisine, Health and Beauty*. It's available on Amazon and I am speaking at events to inspire and encourage others to experiment in both the kitchen and the garden. Writing this book has been a great way to connect with my family and community!

**Gina Vanderham** of Vanderham and Associates, Ltd., is an executive coach and organizational consultant who specializes in mental health and addiction. She has **35** years experience in many types of alcohol and drug treatment settings: private and publicly traded organizations, private practice, governmental organizations, drinking/driving programs, employee assistance work, and substance abuse professional assessments for the Department of Transportation.

Gina is a Certified Executive Coach, a Psychological Health and Safety advisor, a spiritual director, a Licensed Marriage and Family Therapist, a certified Alcohol Drug Counselor, a certified EAP Counselor, and a substance-abuse professional. She is passionate about helping individuals in organizations recover from addiction and mental health issues, and equipping organizations at every level to make a psychologically safe workplace where employees feel belonging and care.

Contact Gina for the latest training programs including: addressing addiction and mental health at work, Mindfulness and ADHD related courses, time management and organizational management, emotional regulation, and media screen time addiction.

**Website: GinaVanderham.com**
**LinkedIn: in/GinaVanderham**

## Chapter 10

# My Addiction in the Workplace

### Gina Vanderham

*"Rock bottom became the solid foundation
on which I rebuilt my life."*
~ J.K. Rowling

I have a passion for helping employees in the workplace who are having problems with addiction or mental health. You see, oftentimes there are not a lot of people left in their lives available to help them. They may have isolated themselves from or have been alienated from family and friends. Addiction is often a lonely road.

Why, you might ask, should I care so much about this and helping others? Well, I was one of those drunk or hungover employees who missed work, or made costly mistakes while on the job. I felt remorse, emotionally checked out, isolated, lost, hopeless, and alone. Addiction has been described as the opposite of connection and I agree with that definition.

Once I started drinking, smoking cannabis and cigarettes, at the age of 13, there were many opportunities for my employers to have intervened and that would have been helpful for me and for them. It's really a win-win situation to address alcohol, drugs, and mental health in the workplace. Lives can be saved, tragedies prevented, and families reunited. At the same time, companies can improve employee retention, attract new talent, improve safety, productivity, and morale.

There is so much a workplace can do to help nowadays because we are becoming more open to speaking about mental health and addictions. Thanks to our evolving culture, and thanks to celebrities coming out with their depression, addiction, alcohol issues, and campaign's like Bell's LET'S TALK, we are encouraging peers or supervisors to address staff with a mental health problem.

Thankfully, some of the darkness shrouding addiction is being lifted and speaking about it has gained momentum and acceptance. If someone broke their leg would you expect them to run up a flight of stairs? Would you blame them for breaking their leg? It's the same for somebody who has been through long-term childhood trauma like parental abuse and depression. Would you expect them to have the same attendance and productivity as someone who hadn't? Hopefully not.

And why is there a need for shame? There is no shame in being someone who struggles with mental health! It's not something that one chooses. Sometimes it is not even something that the person is aware of, let alone can control. Shame says, "I am bad" when guilt says, "I did something bad." Shame is the most toxic human emotion.

When creating addiction and mental health-related workplace policies an employee's confidentiality needs to be maintained in the highest regard. I've heard of a company manager SHOUTING down the hallway for their employee to come for their urine test. They could well have been sued for that.

Is it easy to control diabetes, or is it easy to control a heart condition? Not really. Likewise with mental health or addiction; in fact, the definition of addiction says that there's an inability to control the substance. Recovery from addiction and mental health issues can take a significant commitment and amount of time. Becoming a "recovery-informed workplace" also requires time and a serious commitment; the fruits of the labor will be wonderful. The organization will be safer, and more individuals will get the help they need.

A model called "The Stages of Change," from researchers Prochaska and DeClemente, has proven to be very helpful for anyone seeking to change a behavior. The first stage is *pre-contemplation* where they're not even thinking they might have a problem. The next stage is *contemplation,* when they are starting to think about whether or not they might have a problem. Then they move into a stage called *determination,* where they start to think: how will I change? Will I join a fitness club, or will I start swimming? Will I cut down and try to moderate my drinking or will I go cold turkey? In the next phase, the *action* phase; the person actually starts a new behavior.

From action they move into *maintenance* which means they stay with the new behavior. Or they could move into the *lapse* phase. That is, they might have a slip back to the old behavior for a short time. If they have a full-blown *relapse*, they return back to the old behavior for a considerable amount of time (sometimes forever).

I'm dedicated to helping workplaces create stigma-free and mental health/neurodiverse-friendly policies and procedures that address issues according to the Human Rights Act, Workplace Safety Regulations, and even the Criminal Code. Did you know that a workplace or supervisor can be held criminally liable for an event that takes place in the workplace? Yes, if they have been enabling a situation in which they knew an employee had a substance abuse problem, yet they did nothing, and an accident or fatality occurred, they can be held criminally liable and have to serve a sentence in jail or pay large fines.

It is the duty of the employee to show up fit for work and the role of the workplace to provide a safe workplace. Protection of other employees, the public, property etc., especially in safety sensitive cases is the duty of the employer. There are jobs where safety is of the utmost importance, such as: truck drivers, pilots, doctors and nurses. All of these professions have a higher chance of mistakes resulting in injury or fatalities. In some occupations, and especially in highly regulated ones, monitoring agreements—complete with urine screenings—are put into place.

The point of monitoring programs is not to punish the employee but to protect them and others. I never relapsed in my recovery, but many people do and then get back on the wagon. Because denial is often a part of alcoholism, it is highly useful to have employees on Monitoring Agreements to help ensure the employer that they are clean and sober and fit for work.

A Monitoring Agreement was needed in the case of the Exxon Valdez but ignored. The Captain at the time of the oil spill, was known to the company to have a driving under the influence charge, yet they did not have a monitoring agreement with random urine testing in place for him. The tanker crashed and spilled millions of barrels of oil into the ocean, decimating wildlife, and costing $3.5 billion to clean up. We're still paying the price today from this oil spill, including oil at large on the water and beaches, along with species destroyed from that event back in 1989. Punitive damages charged to Exxon were 2.5 billion dollars. Fines for violations are high and can be avoided with due diligence.

My first addiction was to food and I recall starting to eat for comfort due to the neglect in my home. I instantly became addicted to alcohol at age 13, when I had my first experience with a mixed drink, by combining all types of liquor from our parents liquor cabinet. The dopamine hit was euphoric, and I felt as though I had entered Heaven. It a provided relief from my bad feelings of worthlessness and abandonment.

One of the first jobs I had as a kid was delivering newspapers. I hiked up long driveways at dawn pitching the morning paper onto doorsteps in the crisp, early morning air. With responsibility and commitment, I saved some money and felt good about my growing bank account. Then, when I got my first social insurance number and became eligible to work legally, I got a job at the local dry-cleaning store. It turned out that my boss smoked and sold a lot of marijuana and offered me some. I soon became one of her best customers. We used to get high at work because we worked evenings and there typically were not other bosses or employees around.

Isolated positions like this are prime places for addiction to grow—where there is little to no direct supervision, due to the hours worked or the location. With so many employees now working from home, there is an even greater need for supervisors to check in with their employees around the issue of alcohol and drugs on company time. Such preventative measures go a long way in problem-solving and shortening the time that the disease of addiction has to ruin a person's life and cause trouble in the workplace.

I worked on a landscaping crew for the local municipality. There were several of us who used to hang out and hide out. We didn't get much done if we were hung-over, or even still high, from the night before. My boss never mentioned it, although I did seem to get the evil eye. We'd go looking for groups of employees quite regularly, "Where's so and so?" They were hiding out because they were hung-over, too, and evading supervision.

Back in the summer of 1988, I was 24 years old and in the later stages of my alcoholism. I was working as a receptionist for the city where I lived. One day a customer called with a query, and I answered them, "Hang on just a sec. I'll see if I can find someone who cares." (How rational was that?) I was probably still intoxicated from the night before. About ten minutes later my boss came down and said it was time to get my coat and purse, that I was no longer needed. And, with me in shock, he escorted me out the door!

My response to the customer certainly did nothing for solving the customer's problem, helping the department's reputation, or my boss's stress level. Furthermore, my employer had to advertise, interview, hire and train an employee to take my place. All of these activities are costly and detrimental to the organization!

Actually, firing me was against the law because I had a disability. My alcohol, nicotine, and cannabis dependencies, along with my complex PTSD or CPTSDs, are all classified as mental health illnesses according to the bible of mental illnesses: *The Diagnostic and Statistical Manual of Mental Disorders of Alcohol and Marijuana Dependency*. When an organization has an employee with performance issues, and the employee has a disability, the organization has a duty to accommodate the employee up to the point of undue hardship. In this case, a municipality could afford to send an employee to treatment and return them back to work recovered from their addiction.

That didn't happen. I wasn't identified as having a problem at the job. This was near the end of my addiction when I was using heavily. I remember being a student in my undergraduate degree program in psychology and I went to class drunk and stoned, wearing sunglasses. A turning point for me occurred when I got my semester transcript. I had failing grades! I was also fired from another job at that time. I believe my DENIAL (don't even know that I am lying) that I had a problem was slowly being broken down from these humiliating moments.

I recall going on a date, and when the man came to pick me up, I was already drunk. This was usual for me before I went out. He called me an alcoholic. I became furious, but under further consideration, I realized it was true. Amazingly, up to that point, I had not thought I had a drinking problem at all! At that time, I was experiencing the withdrawal of alcohol symptoms called DTs (delirium tremens) in the morning if I didn't drink right away. When treated with a few drinks, DTs go away.

Near the end of my drinking and using career, I went back to the beautiful cathedral of my childhood. I attended mass and apologized, in a sense, to my Creator, saying that I had become a wreck and I needed help. Lo and behold! About two weeks later my sisters did an intervention on me and asked if I wanted to get clean and sober. I said "yes," as I had been having some serious wake-up calls, which served to take me out of my denial—so common for us alcoholics. I quit drinking, went to detox, and then to a 28-day treatment center on the prairie. At treatment they said, "only 3% of you will stay sober." There, but for the grace of God, go I.

You might think my telling my story is not wise, for fear of judgment and stigma—and that is exactly why I, and other leaders, need to get personal about showing our vulnerabilities around mental health and addiction challenges *without shame.* (We are all vulnerable as human beings.) We need to lead our organizations in creating a culture that supports its members mental health.

I hope that my story has been helpful, and that you and your organization, will continue in your plans or turn over a new leaf and begin to make your workplace a safe psychological place for your employees. Your help can save someone's life!

I serve in organizations to create policy and procedures around mental health in the workplace, and also train managers to recognize and have ambitious conversations with their employees to help them get back on track.

I can help you set protocols in place to solve the problem of addiction in your workplace, and save you huge legal fees such as those based on your negligence of due diligence.

I can be reached at ginavanderham.com, or look for me on LinkedIn or Facebook. I would love to hear how my story has helped you and if I can be of more help.

**Olivia Vo,** The Savvy Social Strategist, is an international keynote speaker, professional emcee, international Amazon bestselling author, and joyful humorist.

Before embodying her savvy persona, and donning her heart-shaped glasses, Olivia held many different types of positions in sales, training, staffing, and recruiting. She is self-taught in social media management, digital marketing, and video live-streaming, and enjoys applying her skills in nonprofit work.

Currently, Olivia is the Development Associate for the Jacksonville Speech & Hearing Center, whose mission is to provide the highest quality professional and compassionate care to all individuals with hearing, speech, and/or language disorders in Northeast Florida, regardless of ability to pay.

Email: oliviavo.savvysocialpro@gmail.com
Web: linktr.ee/oliviasavvypro

### Chapter II

# Happily Whatever You're After

## Olivia Vo

*"Character cannot be developed in ease and quiet.
Only through experience of trial and suffering
can the soul be strengthened, vision cleared,
ambition inspired, and success achieved."*
~ HELEN KELLER

While Cinderella may have been focused on the glass slipper, I found myself rejecting that idea to pursue the glass ceiling instead. Growing up, I imagined myself as the ultimate career woman.

Early on, my parents inspired me to take advantage of whatever opportunities were available through school and internships, and many teachers and mentors exposed me to new experiences. I excelled in my classes at South High Community School, especially in English, history, and science, and that resulted in various college scholarships.

Developing my writing skills helped me win essay contests and being part of the Model Congress Club led me to Congressional internships where I gained experience in politics and public policy. I enjoyed research, investigations, and creating experiments for science fairs.

Any of these experiences could have led me down any number of paths to becoming a writer, an educator, a scientist, or even into public service! Hunger really fueled my young ambition, against the backdrop of the new millennium, and my world would continue to expand when I attended college. As a first-generation college student, this was a significant achievement, not only for me but for my entire family, and set the course for my siblings and younger cousins.

To this day, I credit my psychology professor, Amy Wolfson, at the College of the Holy Cross, for her kind mentorship and ultimate conviction in recommending me for the U.S. Fulbright Scholarship that took me to Vietnam. The ability to travel in my formative twenties helped to expand my worldview. While living and networking in Ho Chi Minh City for three years, I found work in teaching, training, and office management, thus developing my first professional resume.

In 2008, I returned to the U.S., during the height of a recession, and necessity dictated my career choices. My time in Vietnam seemed fanciful and carefree, and the liberation I felt in being my own person seemed a luxurious dream, as I faced responsibility. I scoured online job listings and decided that sales would provide a solid basis for learning effective communication strategies, presentations, and negotiations.

With the sales training, I learned to communicate, persuade, and connect with people. The thrill of closing deals gave me a sense of accomplishment, but I soon realized that my life was being run by metrics and quotas. My true passion lay elsewhere, as I craved personal growth and the opportunity to make a lasting impact on people's lives.

An internal promotion at the company I was working for transitioned me into the field of training and developing sales teams, and helping others reach their full potential. This role gave me a sense of purpose, as I saw individuals transform and grow under my guidance. However, I felt there was more to explore.

Recruiting provided the next stop on my career path. I enjoyed matching talent with the right opportunities, and it was truly rewarding to help someone land their dream job or get their foot in the door with a coveted company. Working for staffing agencies, I managed a full-cycle recruiting desk and covered a variety of sectors in finance, technology, pharma, and life sciences. For over a decade, recruiting finally seemed to be a terrific fit and allowed for my career mobility.

It wasn't quite the glass ceiling that I imagined as a child, more like a sufficient, although sometimes slippery, ladder due to the competitive nature of the talent pool and job resources. Unlike my colleagues who progressed from recruiting to executive Human Resources positions, I felt content with recruiting. The money I earned from recruiting moved me from a state of necessity to one of stability, and it sustained a lifestyle of marriage, travel, home ownership, and real estate investment.

During that time, I cultivated a deep intuition—that "gut feeling" about my candidates and clients. At first, I didn't naturally trust this feeling, due to limited exposure. I also lacked the desire to understand my innate knowingness. The more aware I became of my intuition, the better it served me, until one day a manager called it into question. He seemed doubtful about one of my candidate submissions, even after extensive advocacy on my part. This was the critical moment when I learned to stick up for myself and my candidate. That clashing interaction with my manager, combined with the pandemic crisis of 2020, became the signs I needed to make a change.

As everyone shifted online, the virtual world exploded, and I took advantage of venturing into digital entrepreneurship to forge a new path. In this new era, I could feel my curiosity and creativity emerging, as well. Through the power of networking on Zoom, new colleagues and mentors appeared to expose me to the unique possibilities of laughter yoga and humor. I now facilitate workshops and trainings for schools and organizations on the benefits of humor in leadership and communication.

In addition, I taught myself various skills, delving into the world of social media, digital marketing, virtual events, and online self-publishing via Amazon KDP. It is a dream come true to return to my younger self's passion for writing and to become an international bestselling published author on Amazon. This exciting and challenging entrepreneurial journey allowed me to tap into my creative side, learn new skills, and take control of my future. I no longer operated out of necessity but more from a state of personal joy and fulfillment.

Also, for the first time, I shifted to investing in my personal development and worked with coaches to help maximize my potential. I am grateful for the coaching since it helped me to realize how important it was to identify my core values and personal brand. Now, people recognize me as The Savvy Social Strategist with the heart-shaped glasses and approach me for any number of collaborations. After taking several assessments it turns out that social collaboration is one of my top values, yet I seldom experienced it in recruiting.

Furthermore, having a strong personal brand has given me opportunities to speak on both stages and podcasts, and to appear in magazines. Some of the best compliments I have received include, "Your glasses radiate happiness and so much love," and "Your glasses make me smile." I love that my glasses can become conversation starters and rapport-builders, and I revel in winning others over.

Winning others over or WOO is a CliftonStrengths of mine, along with empathy, positivity, strategic, and developer traits. Until I took the CliftonStrengths assessment I didn't realize that these soft skills could be relevant and business worthy. Others are now inspired by my glasses to find their own special identifiers, whether that's with fun socks, handmade jewelry, hair accessories, or unique custom suits.

Through my entrepreneurial ventures, I was fortunate to get involved with several nonprofits such as: Harmony Mind Body Spirit Wellness, USA Women Entrepreneurship Cooperative, Association for Applied Therapeutic Humor (AATH), and Jacksonville Women's Business Center. I felt very inspired by their mission-driven work and I witnessed firsthand the power of community support and the impact it could have on people's lives. I've also benefited greatly from their valuable connections and resources.

Harmony Mind Body Spirit Wellness offered me fantastic introductions to the University of North Florida, Groundwork Jacksonville, and the Wounded Warrior Project, in addition to various individuals.

The USA Women Entrepreneurship Cooperative (USAWEC) is a unique 5-month, online business leadership and management program run by the Center for Global Enterprise (CGE). This was an amazing program that provided comprehensive foundational skills in business that I didn't realize I was missing.

The Association for Applied Therapeutic Humor is a marvelous professional member organization of humor enthusiasts! Through them, I am enrolled in a 3-year Humor Academy program that takes an interdisciplinary approach to understanding humor, and is supported by scientific evidence and research, with practical business and educational application. My initial love for research and investigation as a psychology undergraduate student is being reawakened as I explore ways in which I can incorporate humor into my profession.

I am truly grateful for the Women's Business Center. This past summer I participated in many of their entrepreneurship programs, including the St. John's Pitch Factory. Prior to joining the Women's Business Center, I felt a bit disoriented, despite the successes I had achieved online. I also felt a massive need to take a break from my digital persona.

I wonder if all my previous ambition, formed during school, was pure and genuine, with a desire to improve myself and create learning and growth opportunities? Now with social media, we are surrounded and bombarded by all sorts of examples of extreme ambition, sometimes all carefully constructed. When you compare yourself to that it can lead to distress and discontentment. That's why returning to your intuition as a friend is very important in getting away from distractions.

Although I had lived in Jacksonville for six years, I never felt fully integrated into my local community because I worked remotely and for out-of-state companies and organizations. I craved social interactions and meeting colleagues in person and the Women's Business Center provided exactly that experience.

The Pitch Factory is a six-week workshop that guides entrepreneurs to bring their businesses to the next level by helping to develop and refine their pitches and strategies. At the end of the program, participants meet with key leaders from large organizations to share their "pitch." It is also a unique partnership between the St. Johns County Chamber of Commerce, Women's Business Center, and JAX Chamber, and is sponsored by North Avenue Capital. I loved the Pitch Factory. It gave me the opportunity to finally synthesize my divergent interests and all that I have been learning and developing for the past two years; it gave me a clear direction.

During this program, a new concept for an independent, self-publishing book business called "The Three Booketeers" emerged, with a focus on nonprofits that work with marginalized BIPOC women as customer segments. The Three Booketeers won a first-place cash prize during the pitch competition and that provided the very first seed money to take this concept further! This was exactly the type of win that I needed after a summer of intense reflection and retrospection.

Another key realization that came to me during this challenging break was the importance of having "frentors." A frentor is someone who is both friend and mentor and combines the best of both worlds! I am pleased to have two in Mila Johansen and Irma Goosen. A frentor definitely strikes a delicate balance between being a supportive friend and a challenging mentor. They have the dual roles of providing me with professional support and guidance for my goals, as well as respecting the confidentiality of my personal struggles and simply allowing me to be myself. They will comfort me during setbacks, and yet gently push me out of my comfort zone, too! Both Mila and Irma helped me to see that my setback was a *setup* for something greater to come.

Both USA-WEC and St. John's Pitch Factory programs were offered at no cost to participants and I want to really emphasize that, since nothing else has been so instrumental to my professional development and business growth as a woman entrepreneur. I am profoundly indebted to both programs and am amazed that they were available. It has definitely sparked a new passion in me to give back and also to explore careers in the nonprofit sector.

One thing led to another after the pitch contest and, after months of job applications and interviews, today I am proud to say that I work as a Development Associate at the Jacksonville Speech and Hearing Center. In this role, I get to do all the things I enjoy and love: social media management, connecting with people, fostering partnerships, and making a positive impact on the community. Jacksonville Speech and Hearing Center is committed to serving Northeast Florida's most vulnerable citizens who need hearing and speech-language services. I'm looking forward to expanding my skills in fundraising, donor relations, event planning, and grant writing. The Center is celebrating its 75th anniversary, in service since 1949, and I have been hired at the right moment to showcase their history with digital storytelling.

When I researched for my interview, I discovered that I share the same birthday as the nonprofit's founding—April 19th. This was a profound sign that I was on the right path! There's a magical convergence of the transferable skills I've developed from sales and recruiting, new technology aptitude, and combined with my Savvy Social Strategist brand and expertise. As someone who is immersed in public speaking, publishing, and helping people express their voices and messages, I feel completely aligned with the vision of Jacksonville Speech and Hearing Center that every individual in Northeast Florida is able to communicate effectively. It's as if the job was made for me!

There's a shift in the nonprofit world, and a growing trend in talent-investing: recognizing that the success of nonprofit organizations depends on more than just program funding and volunteer labor. Investing in skilled and dedicated personnel is equally crucial. In fact, Fund the People is the national initiative to maximize investment in America's nonprofit workforce and they provide a free, comprehensive resource to nonprofits to maximize investment in the nonprofit workforce.

Research conducted by Fund the People supports four key results of talent-investing in that it:

1. Brings skills back to nonprofit organizations
2. Creates networks of nonprofit professionals and field leaders to build the sector
3. Creates a shared vision to drive change
4. Builds relationships with foundation partners and funders to improve philanthropy [1]

In addition, The Johns Hopkins Center for Civil Society Studies released a report stating that, "Nonprofit organizations employ 11.9 million Americans nationwide, and are America's third largest workforce, with retail trade as the largest, and manufacturing as the second largest. Additionally, nonprofit employment exceeds that of manufacturing in nearly half of all states." [2]

I'm excited to be a part of this change, especially at Jacksonville Speech and Hearing Center, where we have professional doctors of audiology, and licensed, credentialed Speech-Language Pathologists (SLP) who are heart-centered like me, and choose to work in nonprofit healthcare. Due to our long-standing history, many of our staff and clinicians are celebrating their 10th, 19th, and even 20th work anniversaries! They are examples of a dedicated team, and are professionals who could get paid much more elsewhere. They love the fact that they get to help our underserved citizens who wouldn't receive those services without Jacksonville Speech and Hearing Center.

One of my close colleagues at the Center is pursuing SLP as a second career, and is working through her credentialing for that, after many years of teaching. She saw the need in schools for speech-language therapy, as well as early education and early intervention programs in preschools, to ensure that children meet reading level requirements for their age. I love being surrounded by mission-focused and impact-driven individuals in their line of work.

Here are three key lessons that I hope you will take away from this chapter:

1. **Embrace change and continuous learning.** Rejecting the "glass slipper" by pursuing one's interests and switching careers can be challenging, but it's essential to be adaptable and willing to acquire new skills and knowledge. Every career transition can provide learning opportunities, and these experiences enrich your personal and professional growth.

2. **Fine-tune your intuition to allow for purpose.** Become aware of the signs and follow through on them. Success and a sense of fulfillment will show up in different ways for you. Align your career with your core values and passions, emphasizing personal joy and fulfillment as driving factors in professional choices, whether through entrepreneurship, nonprofit work, or any other field. Finding your true calling and working towards it can lead to a more meaningful and satisfying career.

3. **Nonprofits are viable career options.** Nonprofit work is not just about volunteering or donating; it's

a legitimate career path that offers opportunities for personal and professional growth. The trend in talent investing in nonprofits demonstrates that the sector is evolving and recognizing the value of skilled personnel to drive social change.

There are research studies that examine job satisfaction and reveal these six factors you can use to evaluate your dream career or profession:

1.  Engaging work that lets you enter a state of flow (freedom, variety, clear tasks, feedback)

2.  Work that helps others

3.  Work you're good at

4.  Supportive colleagues

5.  No major negatives, like long hours or unfair pay

6.  A job that fits your personal life [3]

As you read this chapter, I hope it prompts you to reflect on your own career path and to consider the importance of personal growth and authenticity, as well as recognize the power of networking and identifying "frentorships" in achieving professional success.

In the end, I didn't need a glass slipper to find my true path. I rejected the traditional fairy tale ending and exposed myself to experiences that would help me to grow. My frentors could be considered another version of Fairy Godmothers who give me constant encouragement.

And, instead of a glass ceiling, a new friend, LaRena Major (who I met through writing this chapter) suggested the novel image of a glass orb that creates an outward flow, rather than an upward ascension. I like embracing the glass orb with its feminine smoothness, roundness and curves, and the concentric circles that seem to link the lineages of past and future women. The glass orb undulates and creates waves and ripples of impact. I like being in the center of this glass orb and it makes me feel powerful.

[1] Spalti, Emma, "4 Key Results of Talent-Investing," Fund the People. Accessed 11/13/2023 [https://fundthepeople.org/4-key-results-of-talent-investing/]

[2] Salamon, Lester M., April 2018, "Nonprofits: America's third largest work-force," The John Hopkins Center for Civil Society Studies. Accessed 11/13/2013 [https://ccss.jhu.edu/wp-content/uploads/downloads/2018/04/NED-46_National-2015_4.2018.pdf]

[3] Duda, Roman, March 2016, "Job satisfaction research," 80,000 Hours. Accessed 11/13/2023 [https://80000hours.org/articles/jobsatisfaction-research/]

Experience transformation with **Debora J. Hollick,** *The Smash Through Mentor*! Debora is a powerhouse in the field of personal and team performance optimization. With her expertise as a speaker, multiple international #1 best-selling author, award-winning sales trainer and productivity facilitator, she helps businesses and professionals achieve remarkable results.

Her unique approach will help you create a "selfie" of a different sort, shifting your thoughts and boosting productivity to new heights. In her customized sessions, she shares her own proven research methodology on how Thought = Performance.

Debora is available for speaking engagements, in-person or virtually, catering to corporations, groups, and associations of all sizes.

Debora is the accomplished author of the anthology book *LIVE LIFE IN W.O.W! Nuggets of Wonder, Openness & Wisdom,* and co-author in several other inspiring books.

LinkedIn: www.linkedin.com/in/deborajhollick/
Website: www.smashthroughmentor.com
Facebook: SmashThroughMentor

## Chapter 12

# Cinderella Triumphs Over Office Bullies

### Debora J. Hollick

*S-hare P-ositive E-xperiences, A-ppreciation, and K-indness. S.P.E.A.K!*

~ Debora J. Hollick, The Smash Through Mentor

At the time of this writing, the current state of the world is topsy-turvy, to say the least! So many people are experiencing pain and hardship, some fearing for their lives and safety, others looking for work and trying to put food on the table. Many more are mourning the loss of their loved ones, freedom, and security.

I am one of the lucky ones, blessed with my current living situation and, looking back, my experience has been one of easily finding work and later on business, as an entrepreneur. I contribute much of my good fortune to my parents, as well as to many teachers along the way, who taught me the rewards of working hard and always doing my best.

While finding and keeping jobs were not an issue for me, it wasn't always the most pleasant of times working in those positions. This chapter is about office politics and

121

how I learned to navigate the external and internal turbu-lence that arose during my years as an employee.

## CINDERELLA'S GROWING UP

At fifteen, I started working a part-time summer job at a miniature golf course—a fun job. One of my duties when it wasn't busy, was to play golf with the son of the owners, who was age three or four years old at the time. He had his own little putter and could play very well! We had a great time. The parents had a sitter and an employee wrapped up in one. The little guy had a playmate and I had work I enjoyed. It was a win-win-win, for all of us.

My very first "real job" of any substance was at a hospital. It was a front-desk, information clerk position, offered to me in early May, at the age of sixteen. In grade eleven at the time, I really wanted this job. The pay was great, and the environment very nice as the hospital was fairly new. However, an obstacle stood in my way that had to be overcome before I could accept it.

We lived on a farm and only had one vehicle. There would be shift work and I still had to finish grades eleven and twelve.

My logical mind said to me that if I lived in the city, I could get to school and work without my parents having to drive me. It would have been nearly impossible for them to be able to get me where I needed to be in the short time frame between school, work, and home.

How was I to convince my parents that this was a good idea?

*Challenge accepted.*

My mom often served as a buffer for me when I wanted to talk to Dad about something that I knew he wouldn't be in favour of. Not that I was afraid of him, or anything like that. It just seemed easier that way.

Not this time! She wasn't having anything to do with my idea! If I wanted to have any chance at all, I would have to broach the subject myself.

*Here goes . . .*

My dad had a tendency toward raising his voice on occasion. I knew this just, quite possibly, was going to be one of those times.

Bracing myself, I told him I wanted to talk to him about something I wanted to do, and he had to promise not to yell at me until I finished explaining.

He agreed.

I realized I just might be pretty good at sales, even though I didn't correlate the two actions at the time.

We had our conversation. He only started to interrupt me once and caught himself.

He cautioned me and told me it would be difficult. In the end, he granted his permission on the condition that if my school grades fell below seventy-five per cent, I would move back home with no arguing.

We struck a deal.

Now I knew I could sell! Still, I didn't recognize what I was doing. I didn't even know what sales were.

So, at the naïve age of sixteen and a half, I left home. Looking back, I wouldn't recommend it.

Of course, I thought I knew it all.

## CINDERELLA, CINDERELLA, WHY DO YOU LIKE TO LEARN THE HARD WAY?

Off I went to the big city—actually, not so big—just big to this young, country girl!

I excelled at my job. So much so, that when it came time for me to go into my final year of high school that September, they created a shift for me that would accommodate my studies, as well allow me to catch the last bus home.

I continued with my schooling and working at my wonderful new job, where I was learning a lot of new things — some of them have been a great help to me throughout my life.

My co-workers, supervisors, and all of the other staff were great to work with. Unfortunately, when I finished high school, there were no full-time jobs available, so as a young adult, I now had to find one.

## GIRL GET YOUR WALKING SHOES ON!

We used to call it *pounding* the pavement. There was no such thing as the internet or applying for jobs online. These were the days when you literally walked door-to-door, business-to-business, inquiring if they had any openings. I don't even think I had a resumé.

It took a lot of courage. One had to develop a thick skin, accept "no," and move on. *Next.*

These were also the days when, where I lived, there were plenty of jobs to be had if you went looking, and look, I did.

I started on one side of the main street (told you it wasn't a big city) and, having no success, started back up the other side. I opened a street-level door and was greeted with about 20 stairs, straight up, with a landing in the middle. Other than church, I had never seen such a large staircase! Up I went.

At the top, I walked into a reception area. It turned out to be a law firm.

Taking a big breath, I put on my best smile and asked the lady at the desk if they had any openings. She asked me to take a seat. Next thing I knew, she directed me toward another area, divided by a very long bank of file cabinets. From the other side, I heard my name and a woman asking me how I knew that they just had someone give their notice that very morning? I didn't.

And wouldn't you know it—I knew this woman, although she was several years older than I. She had dated one of my foster brothers!

Sometimes it really is *who* you know, not *what*.

Long story short, I had an interview with the senior partner right away. He told me to come in for a two-hour typing test on Saturday morning.

I knew right then and there I wouldn't be getting this job! I did however, go for the test as I felt it would be rude not to.

*Cinderella, how do you get yourself into these situations?*

### LET'S BACK UP FOR JUST A BIT . . .

I wasn't very good at typing. In fact, I could barely type at all! It wasn't that I wasn't capable of learning it or that I hadn't been taught. It was the fact that my past was coming back to bite me!

You see, in high school, I was a bit of a brat when it came to typing class. My friend and I used to literally put our heads on our typewriters and sleep! Yes, you read that right, I could sleep during the clickety-clack in typing class! Of course, this proved absolutely unacceptable and I spent a good many of those classes sitting on the floor, out in the hallway. The crazy thing was, the teacher sent both of us out there together. Suited us just fine.

I remember telling my teacher that I vowed "never to be a secretary so why did I need to learn to type?" As far as I was concerned, typing made as much sense for my life as Algebra.

I passed that class with a 51% and I believe he gave it to me to just get me out of his class!

And now I found myself about to embarrass myself in front of someone I knew, while she supervised me.

You know what they say about karma!!!

I spent two hours preparing letters and documents from dictation on a dictaphone. I hadn't even heard of such a thing, let alone used one. Oh my. This wasn't going to end well.

Much to my surprise . . . I got the job!

I distinctly remember my new boss saying, "You can start part-time Monday morning for the first two weeks while you are still finishing your other job. Then you will be full-time after that and the first thing you'll do is all of this over again!" My appreciation for the opportunity I was given was immense. I learned so much valuable information that has served me very well over the years.

Oh . . . did I mention one of my perks at this job? On

rainy days, he allowed me to drive his new, candy apple red car to do the court run. Yum!

## ARE YOU KIDDING ME?

I've had a career/business life that has furnished me with a variety of experiences, some great, and some not so much. If I continue on here, I will have a book, not a chapter. So, moving on . . . I would like to share my experiences with the office bullies.

As I mentioned, jobs were plentiful when I went looking. When I chose to move away from where I was living, it became a big step. Finally, I would have no family or friends around me except my roommate who worked elsewhere and was away three weeks out of the month.

I applied for four jobs and was offered all of them! The first offer came from a college, and I chose it. It helps when you have excellent references.

This was where I had my first adult experience with an office bully.

It didn't start out that way. In fact, at first we became fast friends, socializing after work and on weekends. The trouble began when she asked me to come to the college hockey team's games to help out. I enjoy hockey, so I jumped at the chance to volunteer.

At the end of the season, the team showed their appreciation for my help by coming into our office (we worked in a huge space with several of us having our desks in the same area) and presenting me with a beautiful team jacket. I felt very honoured, as they weren't given out very often. In fact, *"my friend"* was, to my knowledge, the only other person who had one that wasn't part of the team.

She became furious with this turn of events! Jealousy green became her colour, and it didn't become her!

She turned on me from that minute forward. She was the senior person in the office, and decided to treat me the same way I had heard she had mistreated others, many of whom had left their positions because of it, or so I was told.

*Confusion* became my word of the day for quite some time. None of it made any sense to me. I felt she behaved very childishly. I thought she would get over whatever annoyed her so much but, sad to say, she accelerated her bullying behaviour.

One afternoon, she decided she should start telling me how to do my job and not in a very pleasant way. She chastised me in front of the other office employees, as well as students who had come in for help.

By this time, I had been in my position for about ten months and had received an excellent performance review, along with accolades from students, professors, and other colleagues. I felt confident I was doing well.

I chose not to accept her criticism, instruction, and berating.

Calmly, I said, "Miss Bossy Pants *(name changed to protect the innocent)* I haven't noticed your name on my paycheque, and until I see it there, I don't have to take instructions from you."

Uh, oh!

My desk mate, whose desk butted up to mine and faced me while we were working, went white. She literally started to shake.

I thought "Miss Bossy Pants" was going to explode right there and then. Her face became fire engine red. I'm not sure but there may have been smoke coming out of her ears!

She marched into our department head's office and blew her top! Of course, I was hauled in shortly thereafter. They were chums and I knew it, so I didn't know if I was going to be fired or not.

I remembered my dad's advice at that moment—if I believed in something, stand up for it. So, I held my ground, stayed calm, and explained my side of the situation. After all, I didn't feel I had done anything wrong.

*Cinderella says, "Thanks, Dad. I appreciate you."*

Nothing further happened to me. I don't know what else they discussed when I left the office, but she still wasn't happy when she came out.

That was the beginning of the end for me. Time to seek other opportunities.

## NEXT

My roommate at the time and I shared a lot of fun times together. On the Saturday morning following this incident, we were having breakfast and, over coffee, were checking out the newspaper classified ads. There just happened to be one for a legal secretary and, having been in that position in two other firms, I was curious as to what they paid.

She dared me to call right then. Being a Saturday, I felt sure no one would answer, so I took her up on it.

The founding partner answered! After a brief chat, he asked me to come in, right then, for an interview! So, I did. What did I have to lose? My curiosity got the best of me.

I had a resumé by this time, so with it in hand, off I went. It was the most casual interview I've ever had!

He sat in his chair, with a mess of files all around him, smoking a cigar. He invited me to sit and asked me if I smoked. At the time, I still did, so the two of us sat there smoking and chatting.

The following Monday afternoon I received a call from him, asking me to come in for a second interview and to meet his secretary. We arranged to meet the following day during my lunchtime. Again, it was very pleasant and casual.

When I received the call for a third interview, I knew I had the job if I wanted it. Negotiations took place and I accepted it, excited to leave the bullying *"Miss Bossy Pants"* far behind.

## BURN OUT AND BULLYING – QUITE THE COMBINATION

This law firm was a very busy place. I believe most of them are, but this one was to the extreme! It felt impossible to keep up with all that had to be done, but I gave it my best. The work felt negative, thankless, yet somehow rewarding, all at the same time. It was a very high-stress environment.

Hard work never frightened me, so I worked a lot of overtime to try and catch up. Never happened! I took on extra responsibility to meet client needs and felt frustrated when I couldn't achieve what I thought I was supposed to. It was a good thing my doctor was only a half block away from the office because, several times per week, I ended up there crying and not really understanding why.

The doctor would ask me about work; I would say it was fine. He knew better. Finally, he told me I was working in a high-level state of burnout and if I didn't speak with my boss about it, he would be putting me in a hospital.

Faced with no other choice, I did speak with my boss. Kindly and graciously, he told me it wasn't my responsibility to make clients happy, it was his; I didn't have to take that part on. I felt some relief but that perfectionist part of me was having a tough time with it all.

I'm not exactly sure when it all started, or why, but his secretary could be very curt, abrupt, and in my opinion, strange. Suddenly, she just stopped talking to me.

This went on for over three months. Not a word. We worked about ten feet from one another. She walked by my desk many times a day. Nothing. Nada.

Just as suddenly, one day, she says, "We should go for lunch." *Whaaaaaat?*

Dumbfounded and shocked, I blurted out, "Why would I want to go for lunch with you? You haven't spoken to me in months." She looked surprised.

Probably not the wisest comment I've ever made.

I'm not the only one she did this to. Eight years after I left the firm, I'm told she stopped talking to the other secretary there for a whole year! She was one of the kindest, nicest people I've ever known, and we are still friends today. Then, just like nothing had ever happened, she started talking to her again.

There's a lot more to what happened with her bullying ways at the office, but that will have to wait for another time perhaps, otherwise I would be writing a book, not a chapter!

*Cinderella has never shied away from trying new things.*

## SO WHY?

Abraham-Hicks says, "Your vibration is where you last left it." This is based upon the Law of Attraction. So how did I attract these situations and what was I going to do about it?

I believe we attract everything that shows up in our experience. The good, bad, and the ugly. Not intentionally, for the most part.

I had a fear and a resistance to being bullied. It wasn't a conscious feeling at the time, and I know now from whence it came. The details of this will be in my upcoming book, *The Bully Lives Within*, which will be available on Amazon in the future.

The circumstances with the first office bully, showed up because of the underlying emotions I had.

When I left the college and went to the law firm, my vibration was such that this fear of being bullied was there, front and centre, like a beacon saying, "Come to me."

It's an internal process to recognize and release these feelings so the environment changes and similar situations cease to exist.

Acknowledgement of my part in it was just the first step. We are all works in progress.

*"To live your greatest life, you must first
become a leader within yourself.
Take charge of your life, begin attracting
and manifesting all that you desire in life."*

~ Sonia Ricotti

**Sammi Turano**, dreamed of being a journalist since she was a little girl, and watched women like Leeza Gibbons, Murphy Brown and Barbara Walters on TV. She loved the idea of reporting (and wearing pretty dresses!) and would often pretend to be them.

Several years later, her dream became a reality. After four years of studying journalism and political science at The College of New Rochelle, and interning for major politicians and journalists (including Geraldo Rivera), she was given the opportunity of a lifetime to work in her chosen field. Working for *TVGrapevine* began as a twice weekly job recapping *So You Think You Can Dance* and *America's Got Talent*. Before long, she was recapping other shows and interviewing big name celebrities on a regular basis.

This led to set visits, red carpet events, and eventually to becoming a member of The Critics' Choice Association. She has been on the sets of many shows, including *Psych*, *Suits* and *Red Band Society*, and has been a red-carpet correspondent for *Big Brother*, *America's Got Talent*, *Celebrity Apprentice*, and the *Critics' Choice Awards*,

Sammi is now the owner of *TVGrapevine* which, after fifteen years, shows no signs of slowing down.

**Website: www.tvgrapevine.com**

## Chapter 13

# Life Through
# the *TV(Grapevine)*

## Sammi Turano

*"Never ever give up your dreams, even when
they're doused in sorrow, because even though they
seem far away, they could come true tomorrow."*

~ Rose Nylund, Betty White's character on *The Golden Girls*

I live in State College, Pennsylvania, home of Penn State and the Nittany Lions. I'm originally from New York; I lived in Queens for the first seven years of my life and moved to Brewster, New York, in the third grade. This is where I met Denise, one of my closest, dearest friends to this day. Denise is a graphic artist and the illustrator for my very unique cookbook—but more on that later.

My early life was very interesting. I was bullied, like many other kids, but I don't really dwell on it, because we all eventually grew up and we all get along now, thanks to Facebook.

I was also really involved in my church and community. I was active in several youth groups, including a video production group, which helped solidify my love of journalism.

Later, I went to The College of New Rochelle in New Rochelle, New York. It was a difficult time because the week I started college, 9-11 happened. It was my first time away from home and it was very scary, especially since it took me a while to get in touch with my family.

My dad worked with the NYPD at the time and I couldn't reach him either. Thankfully, he was okay, but he spent the next three months at Ground Zero, helping out. He lost three co-workers that day.

My softball coach also died that day, along with a few other people my friends and family knew. I was only 17 years old at the time, and up until then, knew nothing about life. It caused me to grow up and look at the world in a very different way. I would have to say that it was a difficult and very scary time, but it caused me to become stronger and more resilient.

I studied journalism and political science in college. I did several internships while in college, including one with Geraldo Rivera, who is one of the most iconic journalists of all time.

That was probably one of the best experiences I had in college, because not only did he inspire me and act as a mentor, as did his entire staff, but he also helped me with my schoolwork.

At the time, I was doing a paper about the Willowbrook scandal (which he exposed) and he not only told me about it and let me interview him, but he also gave me some of the original footage from the expose. He was more than generous and became someone I truly admire to this day.

I actually interviewed him a few years later, when he was on *Celebrity Apprentice*. He and his wife both remembered me, and it was wonderful to be able to reconnect. In fact, I am still in touch with several people from that internship via social media.

After graduation, I had a hard time finding a job due to the economy. I worked retail for a few months and then got a job on Wall Street because, at the time, I wanted to go into law and combine it with journalism. Later I decided that the legal field was not for me, despite obtaining certification to become a paralegal.

In 2007, I moved up to State College, Pennsylvania, and did several temp jobs and other projects in the journalism field. I also obtained a Digital Design degree after being told that digital/online work was the way of the future for journalists.

Finally, my friend Sharon, who is another mentor of mine, told me about *TVGrapevine*. She was a writer for them and told me "We don't need any writers now, but as soon as we do I'll let you know." I thought, *I'm never gonna hear from her again,* and continued working on other projects and jobs, including several years as a market researcher.

Six months later, Sharon texted me and said, "If you're still interested, I want you to cover *So You Think You Can Dance*. It starts in half an hour."

I thought, *What the heck am I going to do?* I had never seen the show before but was familiar because several of my friends watched it. I decided to just go for it and give it my best effort. So, I poured myself a glass of wine and watched the show.

I basically had to write a recap and review everything that happened. Then I handed it in to Al Mellis, who would become my boss, and later, my mentor and business partner. They loved what I wrote and hired me to cover the show on a weekly basis.

Next, I was given *America's Got Talent* to cover, and before I knew it, I was interviewing celebrities on the red carpet, on set visits, and in all sorts of different situations.

This also led to my becoming a member of the Critics Choice Association, which was one of the biggest honors of my career. I serve on several committees and boards for the main show and several of the sub-shows, as well as other events and projects the organization does.

In 2017, Al decided to retire. He told me, "I want you to run the website now—it's all yours. You can do whatever you want with it." He turned everything over to me and the rest is history. The main site is TV and movie recaps and reviews, with interviews, entertainment news, and other stuff added in. There is also a section of video interviews, which showcase several talented people I have met through the years. Every day is a different adventure, and I wouldn't have it any other way.

In my other life, I am a personal fitness trainer and currently have 122 clients ranging in age from 13 to 81. I work out with them and write them programs so they can reach their fitness goals.

Sadly, in 2009, Sharon passed away very suddenly. It took a big toll on me because she was my mentor, and she helped me so much over the years. Without her, I wouldn't be talking to you today.

I went on to interview celebrities like Donald Trump, Bret Michaels, Megan Markle, Apolo Ohno, and Geraldo! I also visited the set for shows like *Psych*, *Suits*, and *Fairly Legal*, along with many others. I was also on the red carpet for several awards shows and events, including the *Real TV Awards*, the *Critics Choice Awards*, and *America's Got Talent*.

I am now working on a series of cookbooks. I was originally going to start a memoir for my 15th anniversary of working with *TVGrapevine* but I couldn't get what I wanted into words. I kept writing, deleting, writing, deleting . . . I felt like there were some experiences I didn't want other people to know about.

One day I told my mom about my feelings, while writing down some recipes for a friend. My mom said, "Why don't you write a cookbook? Tell your stories about your journalism experiences and add your recipes?"

I remember Rex Van de Camp saying on *Desperate Housewives*, "Women who think they can make a good lasagna think they can pull off writing a cookbook." (BAD REX! BAD! BAD! BAD!)

Rex is wrong! Anyone can write a cookbook, but it takes some special spin to make it one's own. That is when I got the idea to base mine on my journalism career and how it all began . . . recapping television shows.

When I recap (or do any story, to be honest), I usually have food with me because breaking news waits for no one, and a lot of my recaps are done during meals or snack time (yes, I still have snack time.) Thanks to my mom and AMAZING IDOL/birthday twin Ross Mathews, I got the idea to marry my two loves of journalism and cooking and make my recipes based on different aspects of my journalism career.

I was reading Ross Mathews' book, *Name Drop,* at the time and saw he had a similar idea. He writes his memoir, and then he includes a recipe afterward that he makes for the *Golden Globes,* parties, and other events. I decided to do it in my own way, as more of a cookbook, combined with some memorable career moments.

I tell my stories, and then I share my favorite family recipes like macaroni and cheese, which is from *Big Bang Theory* because Penny always made mac and cheese. That section also includes a special story about my grandfather. The chocolate recipe for *Dancing with the Stars* features my mom's special chocolate recipe that she makes for every holiday.

The recipes and shows are all connected in some way. I connect a show to the name of the recipe, often with a play on words, and then to something that connects to my family like the Unsolved Myst-ori Sour. My grandmother and I watched *Unsolved Mysteries* together all the time. My friend, Jaclyn and I drink Midori Sours together often when we're in L.A. and it has become our favorite drink . . . therefore, I was able to honor TWO special ladies in my life with the recipe.

The recipes and stories also connect with people I love. From the time I could stand, I remember cooking with my mother. Sometimes, she carried me and let me put the spices in, which is something my sister does with her daughter Aria. As I got older, she let me mix and chop things for meals. She also let me plan meals.

I did the same thing with my Grandma Bonnie, who lived with us up until she died when I was 10 years old.

When we lived in Queens, we had a house with her little apartment downstairs. I would go down to her kitchen, and we would cook together, and she would also teach me how to cook in her own unique way. We would watch *Unsolved Mysteries, Mr. Rogers*, and other shows while cooking, eating, and bonding.

My family is Italian and Lithuanian, and we just found out, thanks to an Ancestry program, partially Polish. I grew up with both parents in the household and a younger brother and sister.

I am also the godmother to two of the most beautiful girls in the world. Isabella is eight years old and the daughter of one of my closest friends, Jennifer. Aria, my two-year-old goddaughter, is the daughter of my sister, Melanie. Both girls are beautiful, intelligent, and amazing, and make me proud every single day.

In addition to my parents, siblings, and goddaughters, I have five fur babies. I just love animals and all of them are rescues and very special to me . . . so they are featured on the cover of my upcoming book. Buffy is a fifteen-year-old tortie cat, who is filled with sweetness, and is often by my side while I work. Sophie is a ten-year-old lab/boxer mix and a sweet pup. McNab is a striped cat who is a mischievous, loving creature, while our black cat Benson is just as loving, but on the quieter side. Opal is a baby Corgi who is the newest member of the family . . . and filled with lots of love and energy.

My cookbook is called *Taste of TV: The unofficial cookbook for pop culture fans based on content from TVGrapevine.com*. It includes 30 sassy recipes based on TV shows and movies recapped and loved by *TVGrapevine*. I partnered with my best friend of 32 years, Denise Maritato, who is an extraordinary graphic artist. She created the cover for the book and an amazing art piece for each recipe.

I'd like readers to remember that you never know when that big moment is going to come, so keep looking for it, and when it arrives . . . go for it. If I hadn't answered the text from my mentor, Sharon, just at that moment for the opportunity to review *So You Think You Can Dance*, I wouldn't be here right now. I wasn't being paid yet, but I did it just to get the experience. I was working another job at the time, and I would just do the reporting as a side gig at first, helping out and not getting paid for a long time. Then all of a sudden, I started getting paid for the work I loved—*the work I still love.*

*"If you take a chance in life sometimes good things happen, sometimes bad things happen. But honey, if you don't take a chance nothing happens."*

~ Dorothy Zbornak, Bea Arthur's character on The Golden Girls

**Jessie Haver Butler** grew up in Pueblo, Colorado on her father's cattle ranch. She attended Smilth College in New England and was on the front lines of the suffrage movement in Washington D.C. with Carrie Chapman Catt and Alice Paul as the first woman lobbyist in Washington D.C. Before that, she helped set the first minumum wage for women in the U.S. from $4.00 a week to $8.00, and worked tirelessly to stop child labor. In 1911, she helped organize the Pulitzer School of Journalism at Columbia University. She later spoke several times alongside George Bernard Shaw, Eleanor Roosevelt, Gloria Steinem and Marlo Thomas.

You can read more about her in her memoir, *From Cowgirl to Congress - Journey of a Suffragist on the Front Lines*, available on Amazon. She is also featured in the book, *From Parlor to Prison,* and is the author of *Time to Speak Up.*

**Website:  milajohansen.com/jessie**

**Chapter 14**

# I Become the First Woman Lobbyist in Washington, D.C.

Excerpted from the book
*From Cowgirl to Congress - Journey of a Suffragist on the Front Lines,*
memoir of Jessie Haver Butler, a real-life Cinderella.

*No country can ever truly flourish if it stifles the potential of its women and deprives itself of the contributions of half of its citizens.*

~ Michelle Obama

I grew up in an unspeakably tragic childhood on a Colorado cattle ranch. Just one week after my three-year-old sister drowned in the irrigation ditch, my mother died. It was the same day she took me into the nearby town of Pueblo to hear Susan B. Anthony speak from the back of a wagon. I remember looking up into her face, at the age of ten, and saying to myself that I wanted to be just like her when I grew up and speak out for women's rights. Some of that thinking came from watching my own mother climb into the spring wagon to convince men in our neighborhood to vote for women's rights. Colorado became the second state to give women the right to vote in 1893, right after Wyoming, in 1890.

I later became one of the first women lobbyists (if not the first—at least the first paid one), at the Capitol in Washington D.C. Lobbying at the Capitol had always been in the hands of men until, one day, the tap, tap of women's heels on the marble floors began to be heard in the long corridors of the Senate and House office buildings. Women went up and down and in and out, urging senators to vote for the Women's Suffrage Amendment, which had been closeted safely in the Senate committee for years.

These women were considered a disturbing element in the Senate office building by some gentlemen—well, most gentlemen. But once the women discovered that they had as much right to be there as the representatives of other interests, they came and stayed.

Lobbying became almost as much a part of government as Congress itself. All possessed one purpose: to keep the legislatures informed on particular interests and to persuade them to support important issues. In a way, lobbyists can be of immense help to a legislator.

Big business engaged skilled men, usually highly paid lawyers, to do this work. These men were often suspected of using unfair pressures to accomplish their ends. But it was difficult to prove improper practices, so for the most part, lobbyists operated without interference.

At the same time, legislation in the public interest remained too often neglected because there was no one with sufficient money or time to provide effective representation for the urgent needs of people.

However, as women entered the picture, lobbying in public interest became a factor to be taken seriously by

Congress. Women, as a group, were concerned with issues affecting the public welfare. They had already won the right to vote in certain states and were practically certain to get universal suffrage within a short time. They were beginning to represent a political power to be reckoned with.

Therefore, it was a strategic moment for the National Consumers League to introduce a minimum-wage bill for the District of Columbia with teeth in it. We hoped this would be a model for the rest of the country.

I had led the charge to secure the first minimum wage for women up in Boston, as my third job, right after helping Professor Cunliffe put together the Pulitzer School of Journalism at Columbia University. We set the minimum wage from $4.00 a week to $8.00 and at the same time, we worked hard to get children out of the factories.

The National Consumers League appointed me as their legislative secretary so I could lobby for the bill. This meant keeping an eye on its progress and trying to win support for it from influential members of Congress.

They commissioned me to study the United States Congress and contact the men who would be interested enough in our bill to work for it. There was nothing dull about Congress. The legislators there came from all sections of America. Even the elevator men and the guards at the doors, humble and folksy, were interesting to me.

No one ever seemed in a hurry on Capitol Hill. To all appearances, everything up there was out in the open. As a matter of fact, compared to legislative assemblies in almost every other country in the world, the Congress of the United States was remarkably easy to access.

Anyone could go to committee hearings, unless for some special reason they were "executive" and closed to the public. Almost anyone could speak at such hearings.

Mr. and Mrs. Citizen were welcome on Capitol Hill as nowhere else in the country. They were welcome in the offices of their representatives. They were welcome at hearings and in the galleries of both houses.

Finally, a model Minimum Wage Bill for the District (providing mandatory penalties for offenders) was introduced and referred to the District committees of both the Senate and the House.

The chairman of the District Committee of the House, Congressman Ben Johnson of Kentucky, was known to be a stubborn old gentleman where women were concerned. He used to badger the women lobbying for suffrage by shouting to them to go back to their homes where they belonged.

He remained the bane of the citizens of Washington, for he seemed to delight in killing anything new or progressive or humane. If he opposed some legislation, it was as good as dead.

"What are you going to do about Ben Johnson?" Josephine Goldmark, who I worked with, asked one day. "You know he has to be seen. In his position, he can easily kill the bill. He will be delighted to do just that because the bill would help women who work in factories, laundries and stores to get a decent living wage. He thinks they should all be at home taking care of their families!"

I relied on implicit faith that Congress would help us once I pointed out the need.

Finally, the day arrived when Congressman Johnson had to be interviewed. The day came, hot and sultry, when I arrived at his office, clad in a bright red-and-white checked gingham dress, freshly starched with a frilled ruffle down the front.

No one occupied the outer office, but the door to the inner office stood wide open. So, in I sailed, with chills rippling down my back in spite of the heat. There he sat at his desk looking like an old bear as he glanced up and scowled at me.

"Good morning, Congressman," I said in a sweet and respectful voice.

"What do you want?" he roared.

A powerfully built gentleman, he stood six feet, two inches in height, with a handsome large head and a great mane of graying curly hair.

Prior to this visit, I had spent hours in the gallery of the House watching this man in action. A man of force and character, who, when he believed in a bill, could fight for it with such oratorical skill and wire-pulling as few men possessed.

Timidly I replied, "I just came to see you about the Minimum Wage Bill for the District, which has been referred to your committee." I shook, feeling scared to death.

"What are you doing here?" he bellowed at me. "Why aren't you home having babies, where you belong?"

A heavy silence permeated the room. The fate of our bill hung on my reply. That I knew.

"Well, you see, Congressman, it's very awkward," I

heard myself saying as if I were someone else talking. "It is customary to have a husband to have babies."

"Well, why don't you get a husband?" he asked.

"All the best men are married! What am I to do?"

At that he threw back his head and roared with laughter.

"That's tough," he said. "I'll have to help you. Now what is it you want me to do?"

Taking a deep breath, I began to speak: "We need you to set a date for a public hearing on this Minimum Wage Bill so that women in laundries and stores can receive a decent living wage. The District Consumers League wants you to help us get this bill through Congress."

I told him that Mr. Filene, who would speak at the hearing, had won glory for Massachusetts by being the first store owner to pay his employees a minimum wage of eight dollars a week instead of four.

"There will be a lot of front-page publicity for you too, if you'll help us on this bill. There is a great deal of interest in this subject among employers of women in the District." I hurried on to get in all the important points while I had his ear.

"Who's against it?"

"No one so far. If Mr. Filene speaks, I doubt if there will be any opposition because he has such a high standing among employers. He founded the National and International Chambers of Commerce too, so businessmen respect him and his ideas."

"What do you do to have fun?" he asked suddenly.

Here was another moment weighted with heavy potential for my cause!

"I go swimming and canoeing all the time I can get," I replied.

His eyes lit up with pleasure. Then he proceeded to spend nearly thirty minutes telling me of his swimming experiences in his home state when he was a boy. He proved human after all and seemed glad to turn from the complicated problems, which must have weighed heavily on his mind. He stopped his reminiscing and asked, "When do you want the hearing on this bill?"

I suggested a date, which he put on his calendar. Then I departed, after thanking him for his interest and cooperation. I could hardly wait to return to my office in the Munsey Building to report the good news to Mrs. Kelley and Miss Goldmark.

On the day of the hearing, the local press came in full regalia, well represented because they had been informed that Mr. Filene would testify for the bill. Anything Mr. Filene had to say became news, especially as his remarks related to local department stores, which were their greatest advertisers. Most of the local department stores sent representatives to the hearing.

I can still see Mr. Filene as he stood before the Committee. He explained, in simple, halting words, how paying decent living wages to women workers became profitable in the long run.

Mr. Filene explained that he, "just a storekeeper," had come to see that increased living wages caused increased demand for goods. Increased demand for goods caused increased production. Increased production put more money in the pockets of workers, as well as employers.

Congressman Ben Johnson conducted the hearing with outstanding skill. The event garnered front-page publicity in Washington papers, carrying the full speeches of the most important witnesses in direct quotes.

The bill passed the House in less than six months, with little opposition. The next day, I ran into Congressman Johnson in the hall and thanked him personally for what he had done.

"That's all right," he said. "It was a real pleasure to work for the Minimum Wage Bill. Just call on me any time you want something done. You know, I have a lot of influence around here."

"Oh, I know that, Congressman," I hastily replied. "That's why we came to you in the first place."

Whenever I hear people today rail against our Congress, I think of Ben Johnson of Kentucky, long since gone. He worked stubbornly for the right, as he saw it, yet his mind did not close to new ideas once you got his ear.

## I Reveal a Crime, Putting My Life in Danger

One day as I was scouting around the corridors of the House office building, the open door of a hearing room came to my attention. Inside, at a long table, sat several members of a committee of the House; to the right of the chairman, a man testified. One or two newspapermen and a woman reporter were off to one side, and the committee stenographer sat on the other, recording the testimony.

Committee hearings, unless executive, were open to the public. I considered myself a member of the public, and so, always curious, I drifted in to see what was going on. I soon found out. The committee was investigating a government report brought out by the Federal Trade Commission to the effect that the five large meatpacking companies of Chicago were in collusion, fixing prices of cattle on the markets of Kansas City, St. Louis, Chicago, and other cities. They were charged with throttling competition and restricting trade.

From then on, I became a regular attendant at the meatpacker hearings, sensing the social significance of the unfolding scandal. At this point, my experience with the Pulitzer School of Journalism came in handy.

It came to my attention that none of the news of these proceedings reached the public, despite the presence of the press at the hearings. But every day, the local papers carried full-page advertisements about the wonderful meatpackers in Chicago and how they processed every vital part of the animal, almost down to the pig's squeal.

So, I wrote down the whole startling story as it was presented, and I then hurried down to the office of *The Christian Science Monitor*, where my good friend and woman reporter was on duty. I knew *The Monitor* was not carrying the meatpackers' full-page ads, so they were free to print any essential news that was worth reporting. I knew that all newspaper editors watched *The Monitor's* stories, making this a good place to break loose the news of the hearings.

My reporter friend fell on the story with delight. I knew the background of this meatpacker scandal from personal experience. Never could I forget the years on the cattle ranch in Colorado. I recalled the time my father's load of cattle had been shipped to Kansas, only to be met with a lowered fixed sales price than promised that proved fatally unprofitable for him. It had been reset by the five big meatpackers before the cattle arrived in Kansas City. Of course, once the cattle were there, my father had to accept the deal. They could not be held there for a higher price except at terrible cost to him. Nor could they be shipped back to Colorado.

It was a keen example of killing the goose that laid the golden egg, a repetition of what had been going on in the cattle business for many years. That year, my father left the cattle business, knowing he could not cope with the unjust monopoly in the market.

So, after that first day at the hearing in Washington, with the consent of the District Consumers League, for which I was still working, I attended the meatpacker hearings every day. I took careful reports of what went on and wrote them up in the perfect professional style taught at Columbia University.

Not only did I share my reports with my friend at *The Christian Science Monitor*, but also with a United Press reporter that I knew well. He came under such pressure during those war years that he seldom had time to attend the meatpacker hearings, so he also took my reports and used them as his own.

Through my secret, well-written articles, the meatpacker hearings finally found their way into the national press. No one ever found out who was responsible for the reporting. I might have been in terrible danger if anyone knew.

It became a classic example of how much can be accomplished by one person when the truth is revealed. I enjoyed myself those many days as news of the meatpacker hearings broke loose throughout the United States. I found great personal delight when I noticed how much weight, even in those early days, the presence of women carried.

With the reports, President Woodrow Wilson, became alarmed. Soon he wrote to the Federal Trade Commission, requesting that they draw up suitable legislation for him to present to Congress, which would put an end to further monopolies of this type in our country.

That legislation was passed. President Wilson issued a proclamation on October 8, 1917. I went on to follow the progress and to report any changes and developments.

### *The Washington Times*
### D. C. WOMAN REPORTS OF "PACKER TRUST"

*Miss Jessie R. Haver, legislative representative of the National Consumers League, and national secretary of the Consumers League of the District of Columbia, attended recent sessions of the Federal Trade Commission in Washington, and will detail revelations of the meatpackers' workings presented. (Short excerpt from longer article.)*

After that, I went on to work alongside Alice Paul and Carrie Chapman Catt as the lobbyist for the suffrage movement when women won the right to vote on August 18th, 1920. Then I traveled to England to share the podium several times with George Bernard Shaw. I later taught public speaking to women all across America, including Eleanor Roosevelt.

So, a motherless, badly dressed, drab young girl with a tragic childhood, made her escape from the dusty fields of

Colorado to attend Smith College, and to find herself on the front lines of many historic events that shaped the future of women in America and subsequently, the world.

[1] Ben Johnson (May 20, 1858–June 4, 1950) was an American lawyer and a Democrat representative for Kentucky in Congress from 1907 to 1927.

[2] Edward Albert Filene (1860 –1937) was an American businessman and philanthropist. He is best known for building the Filene's department store chain and was a pioneer in employee relations. He instituted a profit-sharing program, a minimum wage for women, a forty-hour work week, health clinics, and paid vacations.

"*A woman is like a tea bag —
you can't tell how strong she is
until you put her in hot water.*"

~ Eleanor Roosevelt

**Linda Berry** is a multiple best-selling book author with many books to her credit, including how-to and self-help books, inspirational books, children's books, cookbooks, and several book series.

As the owner of the Spiritual Discovery™ Center in southern California, she offers the unique "Become an Angel Whisperer™" program which ties into her comprehensive book series. As a sought-after coach and trainer in spirituality and metaphysics for over 20 years, she's helped individuals lead an Angel-guided life and offers her fun and informative Angel Whisperer™ Quiz.

Linda is an international astrologer, podcast and summit host, public speaker and presenter, and has appeared on both radio and television as an expert in her field. Her writings and professional insight have been featured in such popular publications as *Readers Digest, Woman's Day, Daily OM, Best Life, Bustle, The List,* and *Elite Daily.* She is also the writer and editor for two international virtual magazines, *Psych News Daily* and *Crystal & Gemstone Teacher.*

Website: www.SpiritualDiscovery.net
Email: LindaBerry_@hotmail.com
Facebook: SpiritualDiscoveryCenter
Amazon Author: www.tinyurl.com/LindaBerryAuthorPage
Blog Talk Radio: www.BlogTalkRadio.com/Linda-Berry

## Chapter 15

# An Angelic Awakening

### Linda Berry

*"Anything can be overcome
with the help of Angels!"*
~ Linda Berry

## When It All Started

When I talk about my angelic awakening I always start at the beginning when I first left Detroit, Michigan to attend college at Arizona State University. My grandmother was instrumental in helping me with my journey which began on a Greyhound bus with 600 pounds of luggage. Everything I owned was rolling around in the cargo hold as I eagerly anticipated my new life in the southwest. My aunt had given me some tattered books on angels and angel numbers that she thought I'd be interested in reading on the 2,000-mile road trip. She was right; they opened up an entire universe I wasn't aware of—one that would elude me for years to come.

I always credit my aunt for getting me involved in a world that was hidden from normal, everyday life. She was an arm-chair astrologer, and this interested me as a teenager.

I didn't get too involved with it at the time because my parents, along with other authority figures, frowned upon astrology. Hearing them downplay her knowledge turned me off from pursuing it. But my aunt got my attention with a simpler metaphysical science known as palmistry. She gave me my first book on the subject—one that I still have today and recommend to my clients who study with me.

This topic intrigued me so much that I did my high school, college prep term paper on palm reading. To my surprise, I received an A+ on my presentation, which was very ironic considering most adults back then were not very interested in this subject matter, let alone approving of it. I soon became prolific at hand analysis and reading the lines and markings of the palm. Unfortunately, this gift would sit on the back burner for years to come as I pursued my education and subsequent career in the "real world" of business and marketing.

Although I would ignore my gifts and abilities in the metaphysical arena, as I studied to become a successful college graduate and future entrepreneur, I did have my brush with the "celestial plane" many times. My first experience with Angels took place when I was attending university and living with my grandmother in Arizona. We frequently traveled from Phoenix to Tucson to see friends over the weekend. On occasion, we would leave a bit too late for the long drive on the lonely desert back roads to home.

I remember the first time it happened on one of our trips. It was a particularly moonless night which made it difficult to keep focus, especially with no other cars on the road for miles in front of us. We were both very worried. I had my hands gripped to the steering wheel with hopes of seeing another car in the distance ahead.

What happened next amazed and shocked us both. A line of angels appeared about a hundred feet ahead of our car, floating above the road. They looked just like cut-out paper dolls, all the same height and connected at the hands without any discernible features. I didn't know it then but they're actually referred to as "Cut-Out Paper Doll Angels."

Our eyes were fixated on this miraculous sight. I'll never forget how my grandmother glued her forehead to the windshield in amazement. The angel line remained a safe distance in front of our car as they floated and led us safely to our destination.

## STEPPING INTO SPIRITUAL LIVING

Although my spiritual and metaphysical interests surfaced at different points in my personal and business life after college, I dabbled here and there but never truly committed. But then, after a strong pull to live in San Diego, I was led to step into it fully. This area of southern California is known for its supportive spiritual energy. I even made a New Year's resolution to become more spiritual that year.

Being true to form, I started a business centered around this profound energy. Bringing all my talents as the promotional messenger I was known for, my Spiritual Marketing business operated the same way my previous marketing firms had, but this time my clientele were spiritual, metaphysical, and holistic businesses and organizations.

Located in the mecca of this almost invisible niche market, my company flourished. I soon expanded to include Spiritual Discovery and started my center, where I specialized in training, coaching, consultations and readings. I not only helped entrepreneurs who were bringing their "underground" businesses to the light of day, but I also grew in knowledge and understanding of spiritual living.

Things transformed into what I can only describe as my "divine plan." This plan was punctuated by the serendipitous partnership with Mother Sarita, the Native Indian version of Mother Teresa. As she personally coached me in the ancient ways of the Toltec Indians, we held ceremonies and group training at my center.

At this point, my Angels were leading the way and I was following happily.

## ANGEL NUDGES CREATE MOTION

My own Cinderella story of overcoming adversity to thrive in the spiritual and metaphysical arena is not much different than many others who operate in this field. It included both ridicule along with being frightened of people finding out about my abilities. In society, we are often told what is acceptable and what is not. Practicing and teaching astrology, palmistry, tarot, and numerology is often considered inherently wrong or, even worse, the "work of the devil."

For years while I made my way through the entrepreneurial business world I was terrified of others noticing my spiritual gifts. I'd been taught if you want to be accepted and make money in business, you need to conform to other people's expectations. I was afraid I could lose my professional reputation or be fired by my business marketing clients.

When I moved to San Diego, it turned out to be the best thing I could have done. It wouldn't have happened if I hadn't been nudged by my Angels. We all have at least one guardian Angel that is with us our entire life. Also, we have other Angels around us that come and go to assist with particular needs in our business and personal lives. When I moved, I must have had an army of Angels leading me to the "promised land." My celestial helpers were having me pursue my calling. It peeked its head up for a bit in my younger years and now it was here to stay.

## START YOUR ANGEL AWAKENING

When a spark of inspiration hits you, it's a gift from the Universe that gives access to tremendous power. Angels make circumstances and people come together in unlikely ways. Most will call it serendipity, or a fortunate coincidence, but it's the Universe and its legions of Angels reaching out to help you whenever you need it.

There are many challenges you've endured throughout your lifetime. Whether you've encountered financial difficulties, health issues, or relationship woes, they've all led you to where you are today. These struggles can bring out the best in you and serve as a testament to your courage and strength. Each hurdle brings eventual triumphs and growth in character.

Now is the moment to make your earthly journey less of a test and more of an adventure. It's time to enlist some help from your Angels. It's time to have your Angel awakening!

Your team of celestial guides can assist you through life's circumstances that seem daunting and unbearable.

Each obstacle you encounter can be reduced to a simple speed bump if you are ready to bring the Angels into your life. No more ignoring them. Instead, start exploring this valuable connection by opening up the channel between you and your divine advisors.

Remember, if the thought of Angels surrounding you is of comfort, then you're already open to having them guide you through life's ups and downs. An open mind and the willingness to connect are the first steps to becoming an Angel Whisperer™.

## ALIGN WITH ANGEL NUMBERS

Seeing Angel Numbers means you are in alignment with the Universe. What does "being in alignment" mean? It signifies you're in the right place, at the right time; meaning no matter what's happening or what it looks like, you're not alone – the Universe has your back.

When you keep noticing repeated numbers, know that you're in alignment. These number sequences are reminders from your Angels that you are on the right path and they are there for you. These gentle nudges let you know there's a perfect plan; the numbers tell you that you're in the right place, right now. It's important to trust in the process that's unfolding.

Angel Numbers are used as a simple way to make synchronicity obvious to you. Most of the time, many synchronicities go over your head and are unnoticed. These angelic digits are used to draw your attention to these moments. Repeatedly seeing them indicates that your personal team of Angels is trying to have you focus on the guidance being provided.

They give you an opportunity to tap into your gut feelings (intuition), requiring you to be positive, get quiet, and be open to receiving information being offered. This includes specific clues to something you're not paying attention to. When you notice these numeric signs, you are being guided in a direction for your highest good. When you listen to them, it validates your intuition, which is why they should not be ignored.

I have included the following Angel Number Reference Guide to start you on your own angel awakening. It gives you detailed descriptions of how to decipher the numbers you will begin to see as you start using the process. It covers the ten primary numbers and focuses on an overall meaning of each one.

You may also add your own intuitive feelings and thoughts to the numbers depicted in my guide. This allows you to create and use a personal "Angel dictionary" of your own. Once the Angels know what meanings you've chosen to use for each number, the line of communication is strengthened and more Angel Numbers will be shown to you.

Before turning the page, get comfortable, clear your mind of distractions, and open it up to the magic that awaits you as you let your "Angelic Awakening" unfold. Let the presence of these loving celestial beings envelop your life in a divine and personal way.

***Author Note:*** I've found after connecting with Angels for over two decades, the interest in them continues to grow. Find out if you're living an Angel-guided life and take my Angel Whisperer™ Quiz at www.spiritualdiscovery.net.

# Flying High With Angel Numbers
# Reference Guide

In Numerology there's a divine connection between numbers and events, therefore, Angel Numbers are interpreted as being signs from your Angels, which represent the higher power of the Universe. The numbers 0 through 9 (including the double and triple versions of each number (as in 11 and 111, etc.) are primary Angel Numbers and have strong connections to your journey in life on the Earth plane. They represent unique numerological messages that deliver guidance from the celestial realm in regards to your destiny and spiritual growth.

Angel Numbers offer support and help build your inner and outer world confidence. They give you an opportunity to tap into your gut feelings (intuition), requiring you to be positive, get quiet, and be open to receive guidance being offered. This includes specific clues to something you're not paying attention to. Repeatedly seeing them indicates that your personal team of Angels is trying to catch your attention. When you notice these numeric signs, you are being guided in a direction for your highest good. When you listen to them, it validates your intuition, which is why they should not be ignored.

The following Reference Guide lists the primary numbers used to decipher your messages. These Angel Numbers usually show up and catch your attention on at least three separate occasions in a specific period of time. It's like a beacon to remind you of something important in your life or confirm something that you've been curious about. They might appear on the clock, street signs, reading material, in a movie or television show, on a license plate or cell phone, stamped on receipts and price tags, and even through technical devises.

In regards to seeing Angel Numbers with a series of two or three numbers, be aware that the repeating digits strengthen the symbolic meaning of the number. This increases the vibration of unlimited potential to the number. It can also add a sense of urgency to the message of the number as well as amplifying its energy to make its meaning more immediate, especially if working through a sensitive situation or emotional dilemma at the time.

When the very long repeating numbers (2222, etc.) show up, it might be a sign to slow down and take special notice by letting assistance come organically from the Universe and others. Another meaning to seeing four digits or more of a primary number indicates a previous planned synchronicity which might look similar to a déjà vu.

## ANGEL NUMBER 0

The Angel Number 0 is associated with the beginning of a spiritual journey, potential, and choice. It represents the pursuit of spiritual aspirations. Its energy brings a state of transition with new beginnings as the center of focus.

Through this number, the Angels are encouraging you to trust in your intuition, abilities and talents. In a deeper sense, number 0 represents wisdom and knowledge learned from teachings and life experiences to assist in spiritual growth.

When consistently seeing number 0 it tells you that you are currently in a strong position to create a stable and rewarding life. The Angels use this number to encourage you to take necessary steps towards fulfilling your life's purpose. This may involve pursuing new opportunities or making important decisions that will steer you in the right direction. It's essential to be adaptable and open to change, identify necessary adjustments in your life path, and most importantly, use your intuition in making transformative decisions.

When you see this it's acknowledging an important message from the Angels. By accepting their presence, trusting in yourself, maintaining balance, and taking steps towards your life's purpose, you are allowing them to guide and support you in your earthly journey. This number encourages you to create a harmonious environment in your personal life, establish a work-life balance, and prioritize self-care and personal well-being.

## ANGEL NUMBER 1

Angel Number 1 is a symbol of change, newness, and beginnings, and when it appears it often represents changes happening to you in the near future. An emblem of independence, it signifies the determination you're exerting to achieve progress and reach success. In the presence of this number, you should be excited about the changes that will start to happen. When seeing the higher vibration of number 1, doubled as 11 or commonly seen on a clock as 11:11, it's a definite sign of new beginnings. You're currently standing at the crossroads of change and whichever path is chosen, brand-new opportunities will appear before you.

The number 1 encourages creativity and indicates that your creative energy is at its peak. Your Angels want you to be enthusiastic about the new changes that are coming your way. When this number continues to show itself, it's a good time to project positivity into the Universe in order to attract the same energy into your life. Having a good mindset will help keep your skills and talents in tip-top shape and continuously drive you toward your dreams and goals.

This number creates one of the Master Numbers of 11, which heightens the new opportunities and enlightenment coming your way. Expect positive changes and a boost in creative energy that you can use to spur you toward new beginnings. Be enthusiastic about where your life is headed, embrace and use provided opportunities to transform your life. Try not to dwell upon previous mistakes; focus on what you can do in pursuit of a bright future. Don't doubt your capabilities; this number reassures that you're ready and powerful enough to fully realize you're potential.

## ANGEL NUMBER 2

Angel Number 2 is a symbol of duality, relating to balance in your inner and outer worlds as well as in your cosmic and earthly life. It's all about positivity and balance and appears in your life when you need it the most because it brings encouragement and hope. The message relayed by this number says that you and those around you are receiving help from the other side. It brings positive energy which attracts like-minded people, resulting in better communication and support in all areas of your life.

There's a deeper meaning to number 2 if you are on a more spiritual path, it shows you're being told that it's time to help others around you—basically becoming an "Earth Angel." You were born to connect with the Angel community throughout your life and you need to keep your eyes and ears open for opportunities to assist others. When a situation arises that you should take action on, this number will appear to you as a reminder.

When this number appears it's a sign that relays a meaning of 'inspiration.' This inspiration can come from an inner voice, social interaction, and from mentors or teachers. Finding peace in your life is what's needed at this time. It's important to create a sense of harmony when making decisions and establishing the direction of all relationships. The Angels are guiding you in a natural way to help create cherished moments and find inspiration within them to live a more positive life.

## ANGEL NUMBER 3

When the Angel Number 3 shows up it's a good sign. The message relayed from this number indicates help from the other side. It brings uplifting energy for you to attract like-minded people for support in all areas of your life. Now is the time to create a sense of openness and acceptance for new relationships, and connection to one's higher-self is encouraged. The Angels are guiding the way the relationships are generated to assist in a more positive and fruitful life.

The presence of the number 3 can signify a period of heightened spirituality and continued progress on your life path. It can represent different stages of your spiritual and earthly journey intertwining at the present time. When it comes up it, recognize this as a sign to evaluate the past, present, and future of a current situation. Perhaps steps are needed to address a problem that has been buried in the past in order for you to move forward without it re-appearing again.

This number may be revealing your life path and higher purpose here on Earth. Pay attention to what's occurring in your life when the number appears, especially if it continues to show up. Your higher-self will assist in aligning you with finding higher power and faith and giving meaning to daily life endeavors. Also, there's help in removing any blocks you have to receiving from all forms of assistance, both earthly and celestial. Results will show in the near future if you take action when the number appears.

## ANGEL NUMBER 4

When Angel Number 4 appears it represents faith in the Universe that what is needed will appear. It brings disci-pline, conscientiousness, and order to any situation. Be comforted that details will be handled and things will be accomplished as you've planned in all areas of life. This number values excellence, so when it appears, you should direct more attention toward persistence and precision.

This number's purpose is to build something of real value by being practical and hard-working. It shows the need for security and structure, being motivated by things of a practical nature. It also indicates the need to achieve what is wanted and understanding the value of self-discipline and rules. When it appears it's telling you that miracles are on their way. The tables are turning in a favorable position and obstacles are being lifted. But, this number is a reminder that processes have to be followed to reach the desired goals.

Number 4 is all about sticking to the chosen life path by overcoming the odds. It indicates that you're on the right path of your earthy journey and heading in a positive direction. During times of self-doubt, this number shows up to assure there's no need to doubt your current path. It encourages you to use your intuition and have faith in your capabilities, resulting in making the proper decisions and choosing the correct directions to take. Trusting inner instincts is the foundation of this number when involved in moving forward in relationships as well as work and career.

## ANGEL NUMBER 5

Angel Number 5 represents change, adaptability, and a sense of adventure. It urges you to embrace growth and evolvement on your path towards personal development. When you encounter this number in your daily experiences, it's essential to recognize you're being nudged to remain open to transformation and continue exploring your path with positivity and confidence.

The number 5 is a powerful message from the Angels, indicating that positive changes are coming in your life.

This number symbolizes life changes, personal freedom, and growth. It emphasizes the need for transformation and adaptation, as well as a reminder to trust your intuition and embrace the process of change for your personal advancement. New opportunities will arise, and you're encouraged to welcome them with enthusiasm.

When you spot this number repeatedly, it's an indication that significant shifts are on the horizon. They may seem daunting at first, but they are meant to bring you closer to your true goals and dreams. When facing these changes with a positive mindset you will see them as opportunities for growth rather than obstacles. Trust that the Universe has your back and these transitions will only lead to better things for you in the long run. Embrace these life changes, as they can be the catalyst to uncovering your hidden potential.

## ANGEL NUMBER 6

Angel Number 6 is a very positive number that brings an inspirational vibration. When you see it you're getting a sign of guidance from the Universe and new levels of consciousness are being revealed. Be aware that valuable insights are coming and should be accepted and used in the most positive manner possible. This number challenges you to release useless habits and beliefs to achieve self-love and compassion in order to motivate positive acts and good decisions in life.

Its overall message encourages you to focus on your life path by paying close attention to inner wisdom being brought to the forefront. The number 6 is associated with the energies of harmony and service, and is a symbol of stability and reliability. When it's seen on a frequent basis, this indicates an increase of its energy with focus on finding balance with a flowing vibration of progressive movement.

This number represents responsible and loving energy that wants to be of service. It's the most generous, understanding, and compassionate of all the numbers and brings warmth, caring and kindness to all endeavors. Being known as a mediator, its main purpose is that of balance and reaching harmony. This number is a calling to examine self-sabotaging behaviors – whether physical, mental or spiritual – that could be inhibiting the harmony of the mind, body and spirit connection.

## ANGEL NUMBER 7

Witnessing the Angel Number 7 surrounds you with the energy of "magic." Be prepared for the best. Good news is coming and positive changes are unfolding. Be patient and trust in the divine timing as changes appear; have faith in what's happening even if you can't see the full picture just yet. If it keeps appearing to you through synchronicity, consider it a sign that you're on the right path and Angels are here to support and guide you.

The vibrational energy of the number 7 urges you to get ready for change. Its specific meaning to you depends on what your current situation is but be prepared to create space for coming changes. This may require you to catch up on things that need your time and attention. Always remember to have a positive attitude and be open to new perspectives and opportunities that may come your way.

The balanced energy of this number brings you a keen intellect and good intuition with an appreciation of the nonmaterial world. It's the most contemplative, perceptive and mystical of all the numbers and is able to study, research, and investigate subjects to uncover hidden answers. Powers of analysis, judgment, and discrimination are being developed when this number makes an appearance, and trusting your intuition and not just your mind is paramount. Finding comfort in solitude can help, this privacy is important for discerning feelings and re-charging energy in order to probe, ponder, dissect, examine and dig deeply to whatever you're interested in – which could include scientific and technical as well as metaphysical areas.

## ANGEL NUMBER 8

The Angel Number 8 when turned on its side (vertical) makes the "infinity" symbol and brings the balance between the material and spiritual world. It represents a mission in life to create a material world that is aligned with higher consciousness. This can be considered a sign of good luck when this number appears by recognizing that wealth or material success is coming from a higher power greater than found in earthly form.

In addition, the number 8 increases the "achieve and manifest" energy around you when you see it. It's extremely powerful and has been widely known to be a lucky number. In fact, it is displayed in order to bring good luck, especially in China where businesses put this number on store front doors and windows. It opens a portal from the Universe, so pay special attention if this number appears quite frequently, indicating a need for actions while this energetic opportunity is available.

When this number makes an appearance, it's signifying that you're doing the right thing and on the right path and everything is in alignment. You are doing what is needed to reach your goals both in your personal life and in career and business. It acknowledges that Angels are helping you with material and spiritual needs. All past efforts are paying off right now as they are giving you support in creating abundance. The capacity to manifest is present and you must believe it, as shifts are taking place and opportunities are coming. Releasing all resistance to abundance is necessary at this time by having an open heart, mind and arms to receive the blessings offered from the Universe.

## ANGEL NUMBER 9

Angel Number 9 represents selfless and benevolent energy that sacrifices for the benefit of others – it's the most loving of the primary numbers. It's highly intuitive, sensitive, and spiritual, bringing a forgiving and empathetic feeling to all endeavors. When it continues to be seen, it indicates that the selfless and benevolent quality is needed in all aspects of life. Integration is required of the mind, body and spirit with the self in order to bring sensitivity and intuitiveness to everyday situations. The Universe is communicating through this number to bring energy infused from all the previous numbers (1 through 8), giving great power and ability. This is a time to sacrifice money, time, and energy to help create the world you want to live in.

When the number 9 appears there's a big meaning behind it because it's the last prime number. Pay close attention to this number, especially if seen frequently over a short period of time. It's telling you to trust in divine timing. What you've been working toward, whether it is life goals, relationships, or even career possibilities, they will begin to materialize. Being last of the primary numbers it signifies the end of a cycle. It's time to rejoice and celebrate what has been achieved – acknowledging the end of a significant situation or journey. Seeing it brings a message of endings and new beginnings, indicating that it's time to move forward into the next cycle.

When this number continues to show itself, the Angels are reminding you to keep your eyes and ears open - there's something they want you to see and know in order to bring things to fruition. They're with you as things change for the better encouraging you to stay focused and alert to messages from them as they bring opportunities and synchronicities in a step-by-step manner. Faith and patience is required at this time to pay attention to signs from the Universe even if it seems like nothing is changing. As fear and doubt are released, miracles can begin to happen from the magic of this number.

## USING THIS REFERENCE GUIDE

When you encounter the above listed Angel Numbers in your daily experiences, it's essential to recognize the messages that your Angels are trying to convey. Using this Reference Guide will facilitate it for you.

Keep it handy and use it daily, especially if you need assistance in certain areas of your life. The Angels are here to help and want to communicate with you but can only do so if you ask for it and be open to their response. By setting your intention to receive their messages you also have to have a way to notice them and track them when they come to you.

It's important to set up a system to record your numbers as they're revealed, whether it be in a journal, in your phone's notepad, or in a computer/I pad file. Make notes next to the number on what was happening at the moment you saw it. Also include what you were feeling and thinking when the number appeared. Pay special attention if you've seen the number recently or frequently and make reference to this as well.

**NOTE:** You may use the "Angel Number Tracking Forms" included in the *Angel Whisperer™ Guidebook* and the *Angel Whisperer™ Affirmations Journal* available on Amazon and at the website—both listed below.

Remember, it may take some commitment and time to start your personal journey of communication with your Angels. Once you pay attention to the Angel Numbers that are being revealed with the help of this guide, your numbers and messages will come more frequently and can be interpreted clearly. These Angel Numbers can assist you in all of your earthly situations – just start listening to what they are telling you. Embracing and understanding the meaning of them can help guide and inspire you towards new opportunities and a fulfilling life journey.

**Website: www.SpiritualDiscovery.net**
**Amazon Author Page: tinyurl.com/LindaBerryAuthorPage**
**Facebook Business Page: /SpiritualDiscoveryCenter**